CW00933155

Where to Go
in York

The cast iron Vespasienne (Urinal) provided in 1866 at Bootham Bar principally for the convenience of the cabmen who plied for hire there.

Where to Go in York

The History of
Public Conveniences
in The City of York

by

Hugh Murray

By the same author:

First published in 2000
by Voyager Publications

ISBN 0 9525392 4 1

(c) Hugh Murray

Printed by J. W. Bullivant & Son
296 Bishopthorpe Road, York YO23 1LG
Telephone: 01904 623241

In the Beginning

Throughout its long history the city of York has been concerned with the disposal of the waste products produced by its occupiers, citizens and visitors. The engineers of the Roman legions who occupied York from 71 AD until the early years of the 5th century, constructed drains in a variety of materials to receive both rain-water and sewage, not only in the fortress but also in the *colonia*, the civil city on the opposite bank of the Ouse. Built in tile, wood and, more usually, masonry, like the complex of sewers found in and around Church Street in 1972, they carried their contents to the rivers but left behind some traces which environmental archaeologists could examine to determine the dietary and toilet habits of these early citizens of York.

Lewis Creed, Warden of St Sampson's Centre, inspects the recently discovered Church Street Sewer.

A Viking Age cesspit complete with toilet seat which had fallen into it after its last use.

After the departure of the Romans, their carefully constructed drains gradually fell into disuse and disrepair. While the Viking age occupants of the city constructed new drains to carry away rain-water from their dwellings and work places in Coppergate, often re-using Roman materials in the process, they used outdoor cess-pits for the collection of human waste. These, when full, were abandoned and replaced by newly dug pits. A large number of textile fragments were discovered in these pits, possibly the contemporary replacement of the Roman washable and re-usable sponges on sticks employed for cleaning purposes. One pit revealed a complete wattle hurdle which may have acted as a modesty screen for its users and in several were found planks with circular holes some 10 inches in diameter in their centres, lavatory seats reminiscent of those still in use in country privies many centuries later. No doubt the precise size of the hole was arrived at by trial and error but, later, in Victorian times, it was said the foreman's bowler hat was used as a template for determining the size of the aperture that the carpenter was required to cut.

From the Middle Ages to the Georgian Era

By the 13th century, with an increasing population and lack of suitable space amongst the houses, there was a move away from the use of cess pits to purpose built garderobes, below which the residues accumulated until there was sufficient to be carted away. A number of these still exist in the more permanent stone buildings of the period. When a drawing office was constructed for the stonemasons of York Minster over the chapter house vestibule in the early 14th century, it contained suitable provisions for their comfort, a fireplace and a garderobe. The proprietors of the museum in Monk Bar, have had to place a notice in one of the garderobes there, which still have stone seats, to dissuade their visitors from using them. Other garderobes, or, at least, traces of them, can be seen on the walls just to the south east of Monk Bar, at Fishergate Postern, Red Tower, St Mary's Tower, Clifford's Tower and Walmgate Bar. The presence of the last remaining barbican at the latter suggests that the contents of the garderobes might be more useful ammunition than boiling oil to hurl at unwelcome visitors to the city.

York was struck a severe blow by the depredations of Henry VIII between 1538 and 1539 on its nine religious communities. The priories of St Andrew, St Clement, Holy Trinity and the four orders of friars, the Abbey of St Mary and the Hospital of St Leonard had all been considerable contributors to the economy of the city. Tradesmen, who had established their businesses on the requirements of the resident clerics and monks as well as the visiting pilgrims and suitors to the church courts, felt the pinch. The many lay servants who performed the menial tasks of the religious houses lost their employment and the responsibility for the poor, who had been sustained by alms handed out at their gates, fell upon the city authorities.

Nevertheless the functions of the city had to continue including that of a public facility, the *novae latrinae, Anglice* [in English] *les New Pryves,* which had been built in 1367 in an arch under the Maison Dieu on Ouse Bridge[1]. Candles at a cost of 3s 4d a year to provide 'a light in the common jakes at the end of Use bridge' were to be paid for annually by the executors of the will of William Graa of St Mary Castlegate in 1380 in return for a grant of alienation in Mortmain from the king.[2] The provision of privies on three bridges in London in the same century gave rise to the saying 'Bridges are built for wise men to go over and fools to go under'! A new attendant was required in 1544 and Agnes Grethede, a widow, was appointed on 9 December in that year. She was to be paid 2s 0d a year for 'keping cleyn the place of Owsbrige callyd the pyssing howes, and that she suffre none to lye any wodd or other noysaunce in the same, nor to cast no fylthe nor other ramell furthe of the same into the watter of the Owse'. This last provision seems very strange as the whole purpose of the place she was to supervise was the disposal of one form of human waste into the river but perhaps urine was not considered to be 'fylthe' especially as public urination was still a fairly common practice at this time. Nevertheless the Council were particularly concerned with the filthy state of the Ouse, a source of drinking water for the citizens of York, and in 1579 required that all the privies and jakes standing on the river bank were to be removed before May 1 on pain of a fine of 40s 0d'[3]. Was this the death knell of the pissing house on Ouse Bridge?

A conjectural drawing of medieval Ouse Bridge. The new privy was situated under an arch at one end.

To relieve themselves of the other form of waste product the citizens of York in 1584 had the choice of a house of ease belonging to a prebendary of York Minster built in the moat at Bootham Bar[4], another against Monk Bar[5] and a third set up in a tower on the walls near to the Merchant Taylors' Hall in Aldwark[6]. Here the waste matter would be collected in dung heaps until there was sufficient quantity to make a load worth carrying away. These conveniences were sometimes called 'coole' holes[7] but the more euphemistic name of 'Sugar House' was introduced in 1658 to describe the public lavatory for labourers and others which had been erected on the staithe. When it was first considered in 1607 the Council appointed a sub-committee of aldermen to find a 'meet' place for it. Its recommendation was that a wooden staithe should be made for washers of clothes at the old place by the water-side and privy at the tower near the river at St George's Close[8]. As the privy would have discharged its contents straight into the river it is hoped that the washing place was on its up-stream side. Be that as it may, it was obviously a well used place as it required frequent repairs[9]. It was described in 1611 as having four seats.[10]

It disappeared in 1731 when it was removed to make way for a handsome iron palisade gate leading on to the newly constructed New Walk[11], described in the *York Courant,* after it was lengthened, as 'This Terrace Walk made on the banks of the river Ouse and nearly a mile long may be justly esteemed one of the most agreeable publick walks in the Kingdom for its great neatness, beautiful town and situation which is so advantageous seen in its prospect as to render it not unlike nor inferior to any of the views in Venice'[12]. Nathan Drake's drawing of a *Prospect of a Noble Terras Walk* in 1756 shows it to be the haunt of the fashionable society in York who certainly would not have used it if they had had to pass the Sugar House every time they made their promenade on the riverside walk. But it was a necessity to the other citizens of York and so alternative facilities were provided 'where the common dunghill is'.

This privy by the dunghill could well have been useful to the upper crust for their needs were no less pressing than those of the common man. In fact it appears that their gathering place, the Assembly Rooms in Blake Street, had been built without this necessary provision for in 1754 John Carr, at the beginning of his architectural practice, was directed to make 'three pissing places' there, one indoors, presumably for ladies, and two outdoors, for the more hardy gentlemen whose intemperate habits would have generated a higher demand for such facilities[13]. Perhaps it was this work, used by so many of the nobility and gentry of Yorkshire, rather than his Knavesmire Grandstand built in the same year, that brought John Carr the clients that launched him on his distinguished career.

Alas, improved times for the stage coach journey to London encouraged the *beau monde* to transfer their allegiance to the capital and the New Walk, although beautified in 1828 by the planting of 820 new trees, was neglected. Thus in 1847 a boarded wooden projection for a urinal could be built by J. Graves on the staithe against Friars' Walls without any immediate objection from the citizenry. He charged the corporation £14 10s for this structure. However six months after it opened, the Corporation received a complaining letter from the solicitor of Harriet Peckitt, the daughter of William Peckitt, the glass-painter, whose house and gardens adjoined Friars' Walls. The solution was not to do away with the urinal but to see what improvements could be made to overcome the lady's susceptibilities[14].

The Victorian Age

The nineteenth century had opened with decadence rapidly overtaking York; it no longer enjoyed its status as a northern metropolis. The changes in habits and manners throughout the kingdom left York without a purpose except as a parasite, a market town for the surrounding countryside. The Corporation had neglected the

Ouse navigation adding to the already high price of coal. This in turn prevented the establishment of any significant industry. Commercial progress was hindered by the requirement that anybody trading in the city had to be a freeman and the amount of capital expenditure within its boundary diminished. Nevertheless the population started to expand, from 16,846 in 1801 to 28,842 in 1841 mostly due to immigration. Out of work country-people still saw York as a Mecca where the employment not available in their villages and farms could be sought. The overcrowding and poverty in the city was increased in the 1840s when the Irish, fleeing from the potato famine in their own country, arrived after a long trek eastward. By this time, however, the railways had begun to provide new employment as well as connecting links to the rest of the kingdom. York had established a new and vital role and its expansion continued apace, the population reaching 77,914 by 1901.

The market, enlarged in 1838 by connecting Pavement and St Sampson's Square with a new wide thoroughfare, Parliament Street, flourished and attracted a great influx of outsiders into the city on a regular basis. This addition to the resident population was the incentive for the opening of many beer houses in the city, a process made easy by the passing of the Beerhouse Act in 1830. This allowed any householder who had been assessed for a poor rate of more than £10 a year to get from the Excise Department, for a fee of two guineas, a licence to make off-sales of beer from his house. The great evil that was reckoned to have accrued from this Act led to a second Beerhouse Act in 1834 which differentiated between on- and off-licences and required applicants for a licence to produce a certificate of good character![15] Beer flowed freely in the city and its consumers required used beer collection points to dispose of their surplus.

The urinal which created Miss Peckitt's problem marked the start of the Corporation's crusade to provide better and more plentiful facilities, starting on the staithes where the barges discharged their cargoes. The crews who worked these boats were usually accompanied by their wives and numerous children so urinals and privies on the staithes were a high priority. Three urinals and a privy were opened early in 1848 on King's Staithe in the corner between the steps and Ouse Bridge. Two years later Queen's Staithe was equipped with two urinals and a privy by Mr Flintoff, a stone mason, who charged £58 17s 8d for his work.[16] But however necessary they were, their users did not treat them with respect; in 1852 the vandals struck at King's Staithe and in 1854 an offensive nuisance was reported on both staithes. The first problem was to be solved by turning the urinals towards the river and the second by replacing the privies with sanitary water closets paid for by the local Board of Health. Water for flushing was pumped up into an iron tank to avoid laying a special supply from the York Water Company's mains. Presumably it was left to the users to pump up sufficient water for their needs, something they failed to do as complaints continued to be made. Then in 1871 the King's Staithe privy was converted into self-acting water closets, followed by that at Queen's Staithe in 1873. Now adequate flushing was ensured but users would have to be careful with their timing to avoid an involuntary douche. A further improvement was made in 1876 when an additional pipe was installed to carry the effluent further into the middle of the river. Then on Good Friday, 15 April 1892, luxury - a new building with 4 urinal stalls and 2 WCs (one locked and the other available to members of the public who could afford to put a penny-in-the-slot) was opened. In the first 11 days the takings were 12s 1d - the public WC was used on average 14 times a day.[17]

The Corporation dredger working at Queen's Staithe in 1935. The privy, built in 1850, is situated in the angle between the bridge and the steps leading down onto the staithe.

While the staithes, a central site in the city and the congregating place of many boat crews, wharfingers and carters, were an obvious place to provide such facilities the Corporation had another pressing problem to consider: the use of doorways and alleyways as urinals by the visitors to the city who came to buy and sell in the market and remained to regale themselves in the many public houses in the streets adjacent to the market place in Parliament Street. The solution was obvious; York was to be surrounded by a ring of urinals, one at every gate and postern in the medieval walls, through which the offending men would have to pass as they left the scene of their over-indulgence.

Bootham Bar

Bootham Bar had gained a new urinal in 1852, 21 years after the removal of its barbican. The barbicans, a necessary part of the medieval defences, proved to be a hindrance to the commerce of the city. Vehicles had to negotiate them in single file while pedestrians, who had to dodge the droppings of animals being driven to market, made their own contribution to the squalor by using them as urinals.

Accordingly Bootham Bar constituted a great nuisance and 'was not fit for any female of respectability to pass through'.[18] So, one-by-one, with the exception of that at Walmgate, the barbicans were removed.

But like the barbican before it the new urinal suffered from irresponsible or careless use. In September 1857 the City Surveyor was instructed to take 'the needful proceedings for removing all further occasions of complaints' at Bootham Bar. His solution pointed to the nature of the problem, an inadequate number of

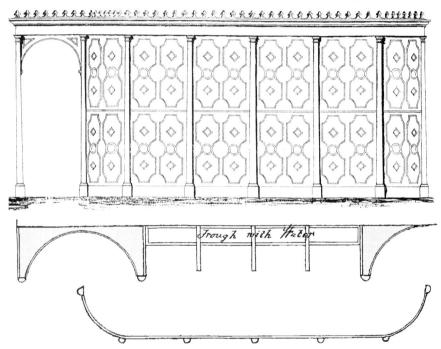

The 1866 scheme for a new urinal at Bootham Bar.

stalls in the urinal. An enlarged replacement would cost £60.[19] This was too much for the elected councillors to stomach so the problem was shelved until 1866 when a plan was laid before them for a urinal with a cast iron screen detailed with strapwork and topped with crockets. Again this proved to be too expensive so a less elaborate screen was chosen to be erected against the wall adjoining Alderman Weatherley's building yard. The footpath had to be widened to accommodate the full 4ft 6ins projection of the toilet.[20]

This new urinal was of the sort made famous in *Clochemerle*. In France they are known as Vespasiennes after the Roman emperor Vespasian who found that there was profit to be made out of public lavatories. He first put a tax on urinals and later ordered that the urine should be collected from all such places in Rome so that it could be sold to the tanners for whom it played a vital part in the processing of leather[21]. Titus, Vespasian's son, complained that this was distasteful so his father handed him a coin and asked him if it had a bad smell. 'No' replied Titus. 'And yet it comes from urine' was his father's rejoinder, for whom gain, whatever its source as long as it was legal, carried no stigma.[22]

Thirteen years later the problem was to reappear in the worst possible way. In 1889 the old Vespasienne was removed because, like the Sugar House at the entrance to the New Walk, it was in the way of an important civic development. After much campaigning the walkway inside the walls between Bootham Bar and Monk Bar was to be opened to the public, the final link to complete the circuit round the city. To gain access to the walls a new staircase was built right across the site of the urinal which consequently had to be removed.

Even before the new stretch of wall had been opened the Inspector of Nuisances reported that the cab-drivers, deprived of such a vital facility, were now using a corner adjacent to the walls on the Bootham side leading to the Exhibition to relieve themselves and this was now in a 'foul condition'. Hurriedly a new, small and obviously inadequate urinal was provided. By November the City Surveyor had produced a plan to build a urinal under the new steps. The councillors thought that the proposed stone screen, matching the walls, however much it might make the

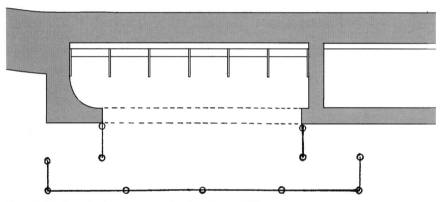

The urinal built under the new steps at Bootham Bar in 1889.

urinal less obtrusive, was gilding the lily so a cheaper iron screen was substituted. The earlier urinals had been open to the elements but a roof was provided on the new one, not to shelter the cab-drivers while performing but to avoid ladies, climbing the steps to enjoy the pleasures of the walk to Monk Bar, from seeing anything that would offend their susceptibilities.[23]

The ladies might have been appeased but Councillor William Pearson was not and he had to pass the urinal several times a day as he walked from his home in Bootham to his office in Blake Street where he practised as a solicitor. In January 1890 he started a campaign that was to occupy him for many years. Regardless of the necessity of public conveniences and the disastrous effect on public health and

The new urinal at Bootham Bar was given a roof, not to shelter the men using it, but to prevent people on the stps seeing what was happening inside.

morality in not providing them he was adamantly opposed to their presence anywhere in York. He could not even bear to use their name. As a councillor he was able to vent his complaint by a motion debated by the full Council:

> In reference to a certain structure built in connection with the approach to the City Walls at Bootham Bar it be an instruction to the Streets and Buildings Committee that immediate steps be taken for the discontinuance of use to which the same or some part thereof is now put or otherwise for the removal of the said structure.

Happily his fellow councillors, who must have understood this tortuous circumlocution, had a much more enlightened and practical outlook and so the urinal stayed.[24]

Pearson was further offended by a proposal from the City Surveyor to put coloured glass in the gas lamp nearest the urinal as a guide to the general public. Imagine his chagrin when the Council adopted this proposal with alacrity and decided that it was such a good idea that all urinals throughout the city should be similarly marked. History unfortunately does not record the colour of the glass used! Heaven knows what Pearson had to say in 1894 when a fellow solicitor, John Hetherton, asked what rental he would be charged to place advertisements on enamel plates above the stalls![25]

The Other Principal Bars

A tradesman's boy carries his basket past the entrance to the urinal at Micklegate Bar.

Micklegate Bar got its urinal in 1852, entered through a round topped arch in a magnesian limestone stone wall on the Queen Street side of Blossom Street. Here too a roof had to be provided as a modesty screen but not until complaints had been received. For 123 years it served the needs of pedestrians going in and out of York.

The 'shadowless' gas lamp stands on the wall of the urinal at Monk Bar.

Electricity has replaced gas for lighting at Walmgate Bar urinal.

In the same year a similar urinal was provided just outside Monk Bar on the St Maurice's Road side of Monkgate. These early lavatories were provided with a continuous flow of water to flush the stalls and in 1865 the amount of water consumed here was 168,000 gallons.[26] No doubt there were notices in all the urinals in York at this time reminding the users to 'Please adjust your dress before leaving' but until 1903 there was no lighting to help the men struggling with their stubborn and unmanageable buttons. In that year a gas lamp was mounted centrally on the screen wall raised on a tall standard 'to cause the least amount of shadow'. Was this to avoid causing offence to those men who could only cast an embarrassingly small shadow and avoid them being ridiculed by other users? Be that as it may the light output of the new lamp was inadequate and it was changed to a more efficient No 3 Kern burner three months later in 1904.[27]

At Walmgate Bar, too, 1852 saw the provision of similar facilities. A tall gas lamp was added later. Strangely, in view of its locality, the water consumption was only 88,000 gallons in 1865.[28] Nevertheless the Urinals Sub-committee thought that this was excessive and instructed that the supply was to be turned off every night at 8 pm to save water; not because it was continually flowing but rather that the residents of houses and tenements nearby, who were not connected to the water main, came with their buckets to get free water at other ratepayers' expense.

The Minor Bars and Posterns

After provision had been made at the four principal bars the next urinal to appear was in 1862 at the Cattle Market serving the farmers from the vale of York who drove their cattle there for sale and drunk their profits afterwards at the pubs which had sprung up nearby and also those who used Fishergate Bar for their entrances and exits when visiting the city. Three years later the next was built at Castle Mills Bridge (Fishergate Postern) in the passage adjacent to the Masons' Arms public house. This was followed in 1866 by one in the ramparts at the newest break in the medieval defences, Victoria Bar, created in 1840. Like others in close proximity to the walkway on the walls it had to be given a modesty screen in the form of a roof. Peasholme Green (Layerthorpe Postern) was similarly equipped in 1878 and Baile Hill (Skeldergate Postern) in 1883. The circuit round the walls was completed in 1890 when the last urinal was erected on the Esplanade near Lendal Tower. The proposal was made in April 1887 and brought forth the immediate response from T.S Noble, secretary of the Yorkshire Philosophical Society (YPS). He reminded the Council that under a Deed of Arrangement dated 7 May 1844 for the creation of the Esplanade, the Corporation have covenanted not to erect any building on the new walk.[29] He was ignored. The new urinal was to be erected in the angle between the YPS railings and the wall of the garden of the Waterworks Company. This posed a dilemma for the company. Should they support the YPS or should they look after their own interests and gain some extra revenue from the supply of water to the new

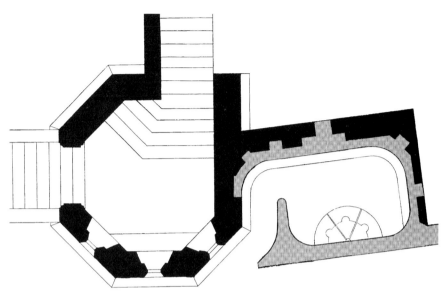

The original urinal at Baile Hill (Skeldergate Postern).

The urinal at Baile Hill (Skeldergate Postern) in 1892. The entrance is just to the right of the hexagonal tower.

facility? Commercial considerations overcame any philosophical niceties and it replied, in January 1888, that it would not object provided that the urinal roof was not built higher than the top of the garden wall.[30] This was not a problem. There was no possibility of anyone overlooking the users so a roof was not necessary. A third objection was received as usual from Councillor Pearson but as he was running an unsupported one-man campaign the Corporation could do as it always did - ignore him completely! In its apparent haste to get the circuit of extra-mural urinals completed it failed to provide a screen wall to cover its entrance. The result was that walkers coming from the Marygate direction had not much left to their imagination. The required wall was hurriedly erected.[31]

The urinal on the Esplanade is at the left of the wall round the Waterworks Offices.

The City Centre

While the ring of urinals round the medieval walls was a necessary defensive strategy the problem of *ad-hoc* disposal of urine was also tackled at source by the provisions of some facilities in the city centre itself. One such site was in Silver Street next to the graveyard of St Sampson's church. The urinal built there was designed by JB Atkinson, one of the principals in what is now the oldest architectural practice in the country, founded by John Carr in 1854. The firm is well known for the high standard of its buildings in the city and the county but not for urinals! At the time JB Atkinson was Surveyor to the City Corporation and this task fell within his official duties. It was obviously a popular site as after only five years it was proposed to replace it by a new urinal and some WCs as well. It was estimated that these would cost £50 but when the tenders came in the lowest were

W & T Taylor	Joinery	£10 9s 0d
William Swann	Brickwork	£14 15s 0d
JR Humphries	Plumbing	£15 0s 0d

a total of only £40 4s 0d. Nevertheless despite this lower than expected price it appears that the improved facilities were not provided or if they were the WCs were soon closed. They had certainly gone by 1896.[32]

Another site chosen for a urinal was Church Lane, Spurriergate, adjacent to Brett Brothers Brewery (to be taken over by JJ Hunt in 1896). It was built in 1857 and served its prime purpose quietly until 1872 when one of the brewery's owners, EP Brett, complained 'of the nuisance occasioned to his staff by this urinal'. He asked for some measures to be taken 'to abate the same'. This avoidance of a direct reference to the nature of the complaint seems at variance with the contemporary use of language that directly and correctly described a natural function. 'Urinal' was not to be replaced by the more politically correct 'sanitary convenience' for another 50 years. Be that as it may the solution to the problem proposed by the City Engineer in 1873 was to build a roof over the urinal at a cost of £20. It appears that the girls who worked in the upper floors of the brewery were shocked by the goings-on inside it.[33]

Twenty years later, in 1892 the vicar of St Michael, Spurriergate, asked for the urinal to be moved, hoping, presumably, that another site, remote from his church, would be found. Alas it was only moved to the opposite side of Church Lane. The lessons of history, however, had not been learnt. The new urinal was built without a roof! This time it was the shopkeepers of Spurriergate who objected - the interior was now visible from the rear windows of their shops - and the roof was hurriedly provided.[34]

A urinal had been provided in 1852 in Craven's Passage, next to the sweet factory in Pavement, as the result of a complaint from Thomas Craven, its owner. The nuisance he had complained of was not specified but the solution implemented clearly showed that market users were nipping down the passage when relief was required. The Corporation was always extremely practical in its solutions to problems of this kind. It had an understanding of human nature and knew that mere exhortation or the making of a bye-law would have no effect. The only real solution was to provide a facility that would carry the urine away into the drains rather than to leave it standing in the passage and soaking through the wall into the sweet factory. Mr Craven's opinion on this was not recorded.

The Craven's passage urinal was at the centre of a long running dispute between the Council and York Waterworks Company which ran for three years between 1865 and 1868. It all stemmed from an agreement between the two parties which had been reached in 1855. Under this the Waterworks Company agreed to supply water for £10 a year to all urinals *as are now or may be fixed in the City hereafter.* This clearly showed a lack of foresight by the Waterworks Company which must have been aware that the population was expanding. It should have had the acumen amongst its management to realise a concomitant of this would inevitably be more urinals requiring more water for flushing.

The agreement had been made when there were only five urinals in the city but in 1865 there were eight and the Council had plans for many more. At last the Waterworks Company woke up to their error and wrote to the Council to protest that they were underpaid for their services. The City Surveyor was asked to take regular measurements of the water use in the existing urinals. That in Craven's passage was found to be using 1,440,000 gallons a year, which was in excess of all the others put together. A special investigation was clearly necessary so a man was stationed in the urinal for a two weeks period to observe how the water was being used. While he was there the water consumption fell to a quarter of the previous rate but on the other hand the Council now received complaints that there was an insufficient supply for the neighbourhood - the residents could no longer take their buckets there to enjoy a free supply. The Council clearly did not wish to abandon an agreement that was so beneficial to them. It was in its interest to keep the dispute going. The Waterworks Company responded by cutting off the water supply. When this happened the Corporation had to send a water cart round to each site to provide, at least, some flushing. A new agreement was finally reached in 1868 which allowed the York Waterworks company to charge £1 a year per urinal with the extra proviso that the water supply at each site was to be turned off between 10pm and 5am each day. How much the additional labour to meet that requirement cost the Corporation is not recorded.[35]

Thomas Craven died in 1862 and his business was taken over by his wife, the now much better known Mary Ann Craven. She seems to have had more persuasive powers for in September 1869 the urinal in the passage was closed to be replaced by a circular cast iron Vespasienne round a gas lamp at the east end of All Saints', Pavement. The outcry was immediate. Nimbyism may be a neologism but its practice is centuries old. The local tradesmen thought that their trading prospects would suffer from the spectacle of men queuing for such a base purpose in sight of their female customers. By October the decision had been made to remove the Vespasienne but practical considerations appear to have delayed any immediate action being taken.

In July 1871 the Sanitary Committee received a deputation of owners and occupiers of buildings in Pavement and Parliament Street, WW Hargrove, newspaper proprietor, John Briggs, grocer, Daniel Martin, linen-draper, Joseph Rowntree, grocer, Richard Houlden, chemist, Henry Lawson, clogmaker, Thomas Foreman, hotelier, and Thomas Scott, corn and flour dealer. They represented

> the annoyance to which they were subjected and the injury caused to their trade and property by reason of the position of the urinal in Pavement and respectfully requested that it might be removed.[36]

The Council had other more pressing matters, particularly the siting of a covered market, to consider so nothing happened immediately. However it had been removed by October 1873 when the City Surveyor was asked to improve the urinal in White Swan Yard to make it more convenient for public use.[37]

A photograph taken by Joseph Duncan in c.1870 of All Saints Church, Pavement, cannot avoid including the newly erected cast iron Vespasienne.

Until the White Swan urinal was improved the drinkers in the city, no doubt, returned to the Craven's' Passage to the annoyance of Mary Ann Craven who like all the other members of her sex had no facilities to use when caught short away from home. At this time women had not gained the vote and ladies of influence like

Mary Ann Craven were more temperate than their working class sisters and would never allow themselves to be in the state of desperate need experienced by many men. It has also been said that women's fashions allowed them the freedom to relieve themselves secretly. In the 19th century women's drawers had separate legs, each suspended from a waistband. Worn underneath dresses which reached the ground these drawers allowed women to stand over drains and perform unnoticed.

The needs of women did not become an issue until November 1880 when Alfred Watkins, secretary of the newly incorporated Chalet Company, visited York and suggested to the Corporation that his company should be allowed to erect one of its chalets outside All Saints', Pavement. He left a brochure with the Corporation officials which described the building as a light and handsome structure of ornamental design in the form of a Swiss chalet (20ft x 20ft x 10ft height) containing cast iron panels for advertisements below glass panels which were illuminated at night. Councillor Pearson must have been beside himself when he learnt of these structures. Internally the building had two compartments - one for ladies and another for gentlemen with the entrances diplomatically situated at opposite ends. There was a vestibule at the ladies' end for an attendant who would look after parcels for a fee of 1d per parcel. A shoe black was to be in attendance and the charge for the use of the important facilities was to be 1d per person, a price first determined in 1851. George Jennings made this charge to users of the public lavatories which he had installed at the Great Exhibition at Crystal Palace. He was thus the originator of that popular, but not inflation linked phrase, 'to spend a penny'.

The chalet would be, of course, of particular benefit to women who, throughout the kingdom had nowhere to 'go'. In London, the Chalet Company estimated, 217 million women a year visited the capital where they were frequently compelled to go into millinery or drapery establishments to make purchases they did not want in order to use the shop's lavatories. Some took refuge in restaurants or confectioners' shops where they ordered refreshments they did not need. It says something about the Chalet Company's view of the logic of women that they assumed that they would buy a cup of tea to enable them to relieve themselves of an earlier drink, thus topping themselves up and ready for another desperate purchase before long.

The Chalet Company had approached Leeds, Birmingham, Northampton, Macclesfield, Stoke, Derby and Nottingham where they confidently expected to receive approval for their plans. York Corporation was favourably inclined to the company's proposal especially as they would earn a rental of £10 a year. But when the citizens of York heard that 'Chalets de Nécessité' were to be provided they had some misgivings. The usual deputation was sent to the Guildhall, this time led by Canon James Raine on behalf of the residents of All Saints' parish. After hearing his clinching argument, that under the chosen site lay the bodies of some of York's Members of Parliament as well as Lord Mayors and other councillors, the offer by

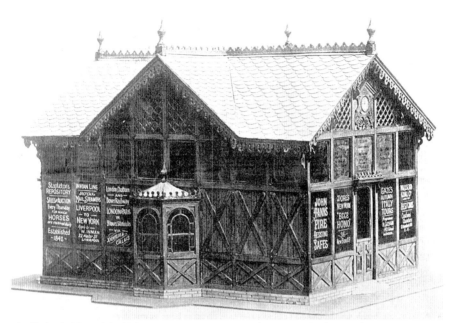

The Chalet de Necessité *which a private company proposed to erect in Parliament Street.*

the Chalet company was refused. Dead male officials obviously had more pull than living women!

The Chalet Company, perhaps surprisingly, had similar difficulties in the other towns and cities approached which surely could not have reached Raine's ingenuity in producing such a cogent reason for refusal. The company went into voluntary liquidation in 1887. One wonders what its shareholders thought of this. They had been promised regular dividends of 20% on their capital if only 96 people spent their daily penny in each chalet. Vespasian would have been proud of such enterprise and, with his powers of persuasion, would have had no difficulty in getting chalets accepted.[38]

The chalet had gone away but the problem was as urgent as ever. In 1889 plans were produced to provide a urinal for men only near All Saints' church 'as there was need for one there'. Amazingly the Sanitary committee asked the City Surveyor to produce a design for a urinal round the centre of a lamp in Pavement - its members certainly had short memories. After four years of discussion, and consultation with the Reverend Raine, the final solution was for an underground convenience with six stalls and, additionally, two WCs.[39] York was quick to follow the precedent of London where the first underground lavatory was installed at the Royal Exchange tube station by the ever inventive George Jennings.[40] The first underground lavatory was built in York, with a single flight of steps to gain access to its hidden depths, by William Birch & Son at a cost of £372 10s 3d. Councillor Pearson had, of course,

An ornate metal railing guards the single entrance to the new underground lavatory in Parliament Street.

objected. It opened on 2 May 1894 and in 20 days the penny-in-the-slot machines on the doors of the two WCs took £2 0s 9d - putting it another way their chains were pulled 24 times every day - a day which lasted from 5am to 11.30pm. Such heavy use required the steps down to be renewed with Mason's Patent Treads in 1909.[41]

The needs of women were still unsatisfied. The break-through came in 1896 when the old police station in Silver Street was being converted into four lock-up shops. The Markets Committee were persuaded that one of the shops should be devoted to the pressing needs of York women. The one chosen was directly opposite the men's urinal which had been provided in 1854. The work of converting the shop for the use of ladies would involve some extra un-budgeted expense but the City Engineer thought that £80 would be sufficient - about £30 to provide the WCs, another £35 to fit up the other facilities and £15 to dig the connecting drains.[42]

It was opened in July 1896, but only between 9am and 9pm on Saturdays, under the supervision of a temporary caretaker, Mrs Theakstone, who was paid 2s 6d a day. By September, however, it was wisely decided that, as women's needs were not confined to just one day a week, it should, like the facilities for men, be open every day. On this basis Mrs Theakstone would have to be paid 17s 6d a week, a drain on resources. Accordingly tenders were invited from those people willing to provide the same service and, at the same time, pay a rental to the Corporation. In October, Mrs Dawson the wife of the gentleman's hairdresser in St Sampson's Square was awarded the franchise for six months at a rent of 10s 0d a month. Only four ladies a day had to use the facilities offered by Mrs Dawson before she had covered her rent but to make a profit her takings had also to be sufficient to supply all the necessary consumables, soap, paper etc. The expected profit must have been forthcoming as she was awarded the contract again in 1897, but now for a year, at the same monthly rent. In fact she and her daughter were the only tenants that the Silver Street Ladies' Cloak Room, as it was known, ever had.[43] If there was ever a case of taking one's holidays at one's own convenience Mrs Dawson must be the prime exemplar.

Hardly had Mrs Dawson established herself at the Ladies' Cloakroom than she had cause to write to her landlords with a complaint. It appears that the men using the urinal on the opposite side of Silver Street were behaving in a way that Mrs Dawson and her clients found unacceptable. Perhaps the novelty of a facility which attracted an unusual number of women to Silver Street excited their baser instincts or their sense of humour. Whatever the problem Mrs Dawson wrote to the Corporation in November 1896 to complain of the nuisance caused by the men's urinal.[44]

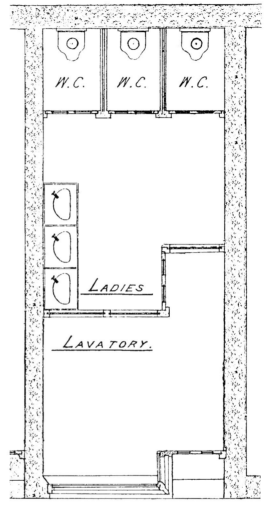

A plan of the historic first ladies' lavatory in York, a converted lock-up shop. To reach to WCs and wash basins the users had to pass through the attendant's room.

The Market Committee, even before the Ladies' was opened, was aware that the close proximity of the two places would cause problems. Its suggested solution was the removal of the mens' urinal but the members of the Streets and Buildings Committee were much more practically minded. A urinal so close to the market and its many public houses was a vital necessity. Far from closing it they considered that this was an ideal opportunity to replace it with a much larger facility! The underground lavatory in Parliament Street had proved to be an ideal answer to the problems near All Saints' church so the City Engineer was asked to prepare plans and estimates for a

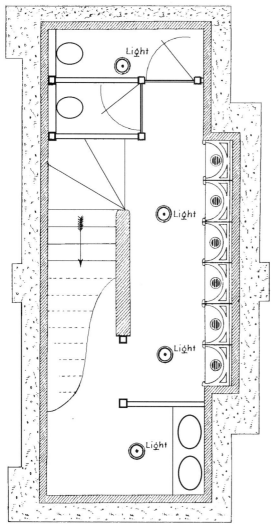

In the new underground gents' lavatory wash basins
were provided for the first time but at the opposite end
to the entrance and WCs.

commodious underground urinal adjacent to St Sampson's church and the footway of Church Street.[45]

Although it could be built for about £400 the Council, when asked to approve the expenditure, declined as 'Parliament Street is within 150 yards - it would be an extravagant abuse of public money'.[46] On just this one occasion the majority of the Council were on the side of Councillor Pearson but not for long. Mrs Dawson's complaint demonstrated the reality of the problem. The Council changed its mind and Councillor Pearson was left in a minority of one - no seconder could be found for his blocking motion. By January 1897 the City Engineer had prepared three alternative schemes. The chosen plan would cost £250 and the two committees would share the costs equally. Only one tender was received for its construction - from Keswick and Sons of York - for £234 0s 1d. The Council were now fully behind the proposal even increasing the facilities from the planned six stalls to include two WCs and 'lavatory' accommodation as well, even though this would cost an additional £60.[47] Lavatory was used here in its proper sense as a place where one could wash. Changing fashions have devalued its meaning to such an extent that the origin of the word has largely been forgotten. The same thing has happened in America where 'bathroom' has taken on a similar duty for a place to excrete.

With the plan approved and the money authorised, the problems were only just beginning. The proposed entrance was to be just opposite Mr Gilbertson's shop. His family had run a newspaper shop on the corner of Silver Street and Church Street since 1851 and the presence of such an erection would be detrimental to the business. His request that it be placed in the same position as the urinal which had given rise to the problem was supported by a petition from 15 residents and shopkeepers who thought the underground convenience would be 'detrimental to their businesses, health and morality'. What can the nuisance have been? The City Engineer suggested that the entrance could be moved nearer the Church Street footpath and the steps down covered with a light roof glazed with obscure glass.[48]

Mr Gilbertson may have been partially appeased by this proposal but the Reverend William Howarth, the incumbent of St Sampson's, was not. The new entrance, even screened, was too close to the door of his church but he was more a man of the world than Mr Gilbertson. In objecting to the revised position of the steps he offered £10 towards the cost of the alterations if the Corporation would revert to the original plan. With such an offer Mr Gilbertson and his 15 supporters could be safely ignored and the construction work could start and it was ready for its inaugural use by June 1898. The hut, hiding the 16 steps leading into the Stygian depths, had the letters LAVATORY glazed into its panels. Mr Gilbertson, in accept-

ing the effect on his business, health and morals, leant his advertisement boards against the hut, giving rise to a complaint from Mr Grimes of Holgate Road.[49] The decision of the Streets and Buildings committee to construct this large underground facility was amply justified. It became the most popular calling point for men in York. In

The shelter over the entrance to the underground gents' lavatory in Silver street has the letters 'LAVATORY' painted on the glass while the lamppost directs users to the 'Mens' Lavatory'.

1913 when there were 10 WCs in the city the income for the financial year from Silver Street was £47 13s 1d out of a total of £132 12s 3d - 31 daily pulls of the chain out of 87 city wide.[50] The responsibility of collecting the takings at this time fell to the hard-worked City Police Force whose duties included, amongst the normally expected duties of directing traffic and preventing crime, fighting fires and observing the electric street lights to check that they were all working.

The Suburbs

Having ensured that no man could leave the walled city without passing a urinal, the Corporation's policy for the suburbs seems to have been to respond to demand, both from potential users of the facilities and those who found them objectionable. The various barracks and other military establishments on Fulford Road generated a considerable flow of soldiers into and out of the city, especially at the weekends. The city destination of the troops was, of course, the many drinking establishments there. Their return journey would thus be marked by many comfort stops in lanes and alleys, gardens and doorways. There was a clear need to provide an official urinal to supplant all the *ad-hoc* arrangements and what better place than the small triangle of land outside the Conservative Club in the angle between Fishergate and Cemetery Road, half way between the city and the barracks. This had earlier been planted with trees and shrubs which must have already provided cover for the relief

The urinal on the triangular site in front of Fulford Conservative Club served not only the soldiers returning to barracks but waiting passengers at the horse drawn tram stop at the passing loop.

activities of the soldiers. For a time, after the erection of the new urinal, all went well but in October 1888 the City Surveyor asked if he could remove it. It appears that political pressure was greater than bladder pressure![51]

Removal of a facility did not mean that the use of its site for relief purposes would cease. Wiser counsels resulted in the building of two substitute facilities on the soldier's itineraries. A six-stall urinal was placed in the triangular enclosure at the junction of Fishergate and Fawcett Street. It cost £50 and only one tree had to be sacrificed to make way for it. The second was to be strategically placed on the city side of the Barrack Tavern (Fulford Arms).[52] But the lessons of history were again not learnt. In 1910 a plan was prepared for a urinal on the triangular piece of land at the junction of Cemetery Road and Fulford Road. That the City Engineer was aware of its location, if not the sensitivity of the site, is shown by the inclusion of the words 'immediately opposite Fulford Conservative Club' in his description of the place where he intended to erect it.[53]

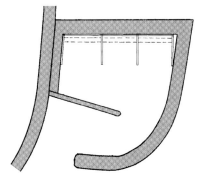

While Fishergate and Fulford Road was the main route between the city and the barracks, some soldiers used the alternative riverside New Walk. A three-stall stone urinal at Blue Bridge, similar to that already erected on the Esplanade, would cost, including drainage, £28 while a supply of water, if obtained from Sandringham Terrace would require an extra £7 or from Marlborough Grove £8. After a visit from the Urinals Sub-Committee it was decided that the most suitable site was in Blue Bridge Lane between the iron entrance gate to New Walk and the wall of York High School for Girls which had just opened in Fishergate House. The fixing of a gas lamp over the urinal represented the cherry on the icing! By siting the urinal just off the line of New Walk the committee had avoided making an eyesore in the grand design of their 18th century predecessors.[54]

The urinal in Blue Bridge Lane was equipped with three slate stalls.

Another place where there was a large concentration of men was in the Township of Holgate, where the North Eastern Railway had established its Carriage and Wagon Works. Hundreds of men worked there and there was no suitable provision between Micklegate Bar and the city boundary, a distance of 1½ miles - a slight exaggeration by the petitioners from the township wanting to strengthen their case. Luckily the Corporation owned a small piece of land on the Holgate side of Holgate Beck next to the gateway leading to one of Backhouse's fields. In spite of the accustomed objection from Councillor Pearson a tender of £62 11s 9d from William Birch and Son was accepted and the urinal was available for the relief of Holgate in 1895.[55]

At the same time the entrance to the Island, an estate of isolated terraced houses at the end of Leeman Road was marked by the provision of a urinal in Kingsland Terrace against the abutment of the railway bridge. Two years later, in 1897, the NER woke up to the fact that this urinal obstructed its frontage rights and it had, in fact, been built on land which it had conveyed to the Corporation for street and not building purposes. The NER's claim for the very reasonable rent of 1s 0d a year and the right to have the urinal removed at any time they requested it was obviously designed to protect its interests without offending the Corporation. The Corporation on its part was happy to accept this compromise without any haggling.[56]

Improvements

In the first half of the 19th century the urinals and WCs, which had drains, were connected to sewers which discharged their effluent in the nearest river, the Ouse or the Foss. The main purpose of these sewers was to carry away storm water from the streets with the consequence that stagnant slop water, urine and other matter accumulated in the courts in which people lived. Manure was carried from middens of the houses by night soil men who left their foul gatherings in heaps in the poorer riverside areas of York until they had sufficient to make a barge load which was then sent away by river to farms outside the city. Neither were the gutters and sewers properly flushed. This state of things, of course, was a considerable health hazard. In a first attempt to improve matters four major sewers were constructed in 1850 by the Commissioners of Paving etc., one running along each bank of the two rivers. Their purpose was to capture all the drains which ran from streets and buildings directly to the rivers and then to carry the foul matter to a point below the city where it would no longer be detrimental to the well-being of the majority of York citizens, however much it might be objectionable to towns like Selby and Goole further downstream. The sewer on the south bank discharged into the Ouse at the end of Clementhorpe while all the rest liberated their contents into the Foss in Browney Dike below Castle Mills dam. This dam was a significant contributor to the unhealthiness of the areas alongside the Foss as it prevented vegetable and animal matter thrown into the river from flowing away.[57] After the sewers were built there was a gradual improvement in the death rate in the city. In the early years of the century this had been 30 or more deaths per year per 1,000 population but after the provision of the sewers it fell to 20 by 1890.

Further improvements in the death rate were occasioned by the opening of Naburn Sewage Treatment Works in 1892. By this time many houses had flush WCs and their contents, together with rainwater, were pumped away from the city to Naburn where it could be treated. Here the liquid is filtered and cleaned before being discharged into the Ouse and the solid matter accumulates in settling tanks from which it can be carted away to nearby farms as fertilizer. Again the effect on the death rate was easily discernible, falling from 20 deaths per year per 1000 population at the opening of the sewage works to 12 by 1920. Since then, with all the great advances in medical science, the death rate has only improved marginally to 11. Proper disposal of sewage, then, has been the greatest contributor to public health; something which was known by the Greeks and Romans but which has had to be laboriously and expensively relearnt by their successors.

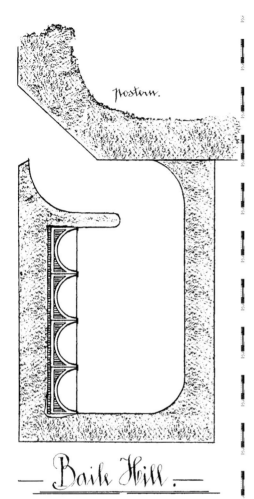

The proposed layout of porcelain stalls to replace the earlier semi-circular trough.

All the stalls in the early urinals were simple upright slate slabs. While they had served their original purpose they were, at the end of the 19th century, considered to be old and insanitary. In 1899 the City Engineer proposed to replace them with new porcelain stalls. He obtained estimates from three firms; Adams of York, Oates & Green of Halifax and Ducketts of Burnley. Obviously there was little to choose between the prices of the three firms so the councillors instructed their engineer to obtain a sample stall from each which was to be erected at the Corporation depot in Foss Islands for them to inspect. One has a vision of the committee first calling in at the John Bull in Layerthorpe to make sure they were fully equipped for their task! What criteria they used in reaching their decision is not known but the immediate result, in February 1900, was that it was decided to accept Ducketts's tender of £201.[58] However it seems that the best efforts of the committee in testing the trial stalls were considered to be less than adequate for on 18 December 1900 only seven stalls for Victoria Bar were ordered from Ducketts. At the same time eight stalls for Micklegate Bar were ordered from Adams and seven stalls for Monk Bar from Oates and Green. The great urinal-using public were obviously thought to be far better equipped to give the new stalls a proper test than the more sober committee. While waiting for the outcome of the second test the City Engineer arranged to have all the public urinals disinfected. In the end the first opinions of the committee were proved to be right and Ducketts were given the contract in October 1902 to supply a further 24 stalls for £67 12s 0d.[59]

In submitting their tenders to a civic authority it is unlikely that any of these suppliers would have included in their price an item for a bull's eye target or a bee under the glaze of the new stalls. These devices were placed at a spot, carefully

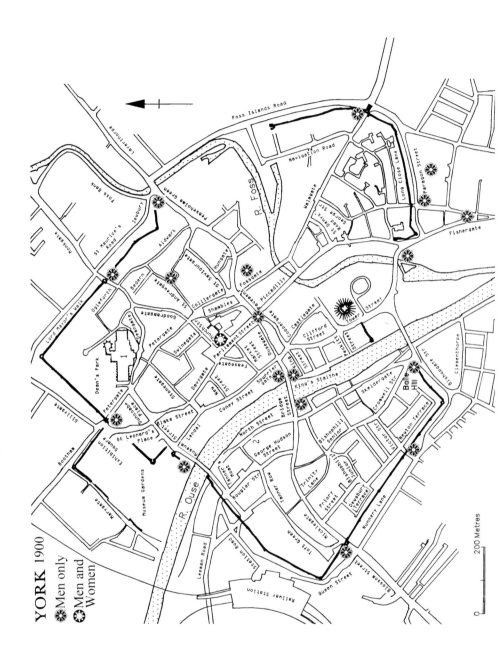

YORK 1900

● Men only

✳ Men and Women

Lendal Bridge

Foss Bank

Monkgate

St Maurice's Road

Layerthorpe

R. FOSS

Foss Islands Road

Navigation Road

Walmgate

Long Close Lane

George Str

Parsman Street

St Denys Road

George Str

Fishergate

Peasholme Green

Aldwark

Hungate

Jewbury

St Andrewgate

St Saviourgate

Fossgate

Colliergate

Shambles

Piccadilly

Merchantgate

Copergate

Castlegate

Tower Street

Clifford Street

Dixon Lane

Friargate

Clementhorpe

Bishopgate Str

Lord Mayor's Walk

Ogleforth

Bedern

Goodramgate

Petergate

Swinegate

Stonegate

Grape Lane

Deangate

Dean's Park

Minster Yard

Assize Court

Parliament Street

Jubbergate

Market Street

Feasegate

Coney Street

Spurrier Gate

Nessgate

Low Ousegate

High Ousegate

Coppergate

King's Staithe

Bridge Street

North Street

Skeldergate

Cromwell Str

Baile Hill

Newton Terrace

Victor Str

Precentor's Court

Bootham

Exhibition Square

St Leonard's Place

Duncombe Place

Minster Gates

Blake Street

Museum Street

Lendal

Museum Gardens

R. OUSE

St Helen's Square

George Hudson Street

Tanner Row

Rougier Street

Trinity Lane

Priory Street

Bishophill Senior

Bishophill Junior

Fetter Lane

Queen Street

Micklegate

Ovesbury Terrace

Nunnery Lane

Fort Green

Marygate

Lendal Road

Station Road

Station Rise

Railway Station

Blossom Street

Queen Street

Leeman Road

200 Metres

0

calculated by the laws of ballistics, which, if the men aimed at it, would ensure that they did not splash their boots while performing. The choice of a bee was especially significant - the Latin for a bee is *apis*. [60]

The Premises, 1900

As the nineteenth century closed, York could boast many micturition facilities for men, only a few male WCs and just one place where women could 'go'. The requirement for men to wash their hands after performing was obviously not considered to be a necessity as only one facility was provided with wash-hand basins. Ladies on the other hand had a 100% provision - one basin per WC.

Wcs	First provided
Silver Street - Ladies Cloak Room (plus three wash-hand basins)	1896

Wcs and Urinals	
King's Staithe (automatic flush)	1847
Parliament Street	1894
Silver Street (plus two wash-hand basins)	1898

Urinals only	
Baile Hill (Skeldergate Postern)	1883
Black Horse Passage	1884
Blue Bridge Lane	1888
Bootham Bar	1852
Castle Mills Bridge (Fishergate Postern)	1855
Church Lane, Spurriergate	1857
Fawcett Street (Cattle Market & Fishergate Bar)	1862
Fishergate	1890
Foss Bridge	1852
Holgate Road	1895
Leeman Road (Kingsland Terrace)	1897
Lendal Bridge (Esplanade)	1887
Monk Bar	1852
Peasholme Green Bridge (Layerthorpe Postern)	1878
Queen's Staithe	1850
St Andrewgate Churchyard	1866
Tower Street	
Victoria Bar	1866
Walmgate Pig Market	1881
Walmgate Bar	1852

FOR RAISING SEWAGE AUTOMATICALLY
Use ADAMS'
PATENT SEWAGE LIFT.

ADAMS' PATENT LIFT CO.,
ENGINEERS,
5 & 7, OLD QUEEN STREET,
WESTMINSTER, LONDON.
And YORK.

SEWAGE RAISED

SEWAGE TO BE RAISED

ADAMS' PAT SEWAGE LIFT

Makers of
FLUSHING SYPHONS,
SLUICES, &c.

DUCKETTS'
WASH-DOWN PEDESTAL CLOSET,

"THE CLENCHER."

SELF-CONTAINED—HEAVY—STRONG.

AWARDED THE **BRONZE MEDAL**
OF THE SANITARY INSTITUTE,
LEEDS EXHIBITION, 1897.

Prices and Particulars on application to the Patentees and Manufacturers—
J. DUCKETT & SON, Ld., Sanitary Ware Works,
BURNLEY, Lancashire.

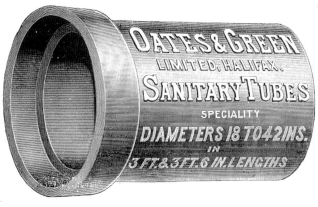

OATES & GREEN
LIMITED, HALIFAX.
SANITARY TUBES
SPECIALITY
DIAMETERS 18 TO 42 INS.
IN
3 FT. & 3 FT. 6 IN. LENGTHS

WHITE, COLOURED AND
SPECIAL SALT
GLAZED
BRICKS
OF THE
HIGHEST QUALITY.

OATES & GREEN,
LIMITED,
HALIFAX.

STANFORD JOINTED
PIPES A SPECIALITY.

The Twentieth Century

Seebohm Rowntree's survey in 1900 of poverty in York revealed that there were 338 licensed premises serving a population of 77793, one licence for every 230 citizens regardless of age. The majority of these were for the consumption of drink on the premises, 199 fully licensed and 37 for beer only, a total of 236. There were also 102 'off licences', 27 for wines and spirits and 75 for beer. With this number of drink purveyors York was slightly above average. At the top of the league was Northampton with one licence for every 167 people and at the opposite extreme was Cardiff where the comparative figure was 458.[61]

At this time there were no licensing hours; these were not introduced until 1921. The tenants of public houses and 'off licences' could stay open for as long as they thought it beneficial to their businesses and their profits. The opportunity for the drinking classes in York to fill their bladders was unrestricted in both time and place. The need for an adequate provision of places where they could relieve themselves of the volume effects of their consumption, if not of the alcoholic effects, was paramount. The Corporation could not afford to be complacent. The situation needed to be kept under review, new sites found, some old sites improved and others, that were no longer viable, closed.

Consolidation and Improvements

New building developments also required the closure or resiting of a convenience. The five stall installation in the alley-way adjacent to the Mason's Arms in Fishergate was in the way of a new building that H. Foster & Son, builders' merchants, wished to build between the public house and the River Foss. A new urinal built nearby would cost about £200 but Fosters offered to pay £20 if they were allowed to incorporate the old site into their new building. This, of course, meant that there would be no replacement facility, a possibility which was an anathema to R. Dutton, a rival builders' merchant on the upstream side of Castle Mills Bridge, whose staff would have had to waste more time finding a place to spend their pennies. As a result of Dutton's objection a new site was chosen in the plantation between St George's Field and the river where a new building with both stalls and two WCs could be built for men only.[62]

At the beginning of the new century York did not have a public park where those living in crowded terraces could take healthy walks amongst lawns, flowers and shrubs and breathe the relatively uncontaminated air to be found there. Haxby Road was selected to lead the way and a small triangle of land at the junction with Wigginton Road, previously used for market gardens, had been chosen in 1898. A plan of its layout was not produced until January 1900 and even then did not include any public conveniences but by the time the new park was informally opened on Whit Monday, 19 May 1902, George Naylor had erected a urinal and WCs (also called a sanitary convenience - one of the earliest uses of this appellation in York) in the corner of the site nearest Clarence Street at a cost of £366 1s 0½d. Either vandals or water stealers became an immediate problem as the beat policeman on duty in the neighbourhood was required to lock it up every day on the first occasion he passed it after 11.00pm. In April 1913 a building containing 2 WCs for ladies' use was erected alongside the Gents' but inside the park. The Gents' could not be reached from within the park. Male users, in a hurry or not, had to take a circuitous route for relief. In was not until 1925 that alterations were made at a cost of £14 to allow direct access from the park.[63]

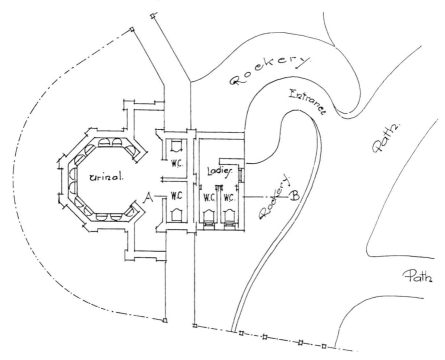

Twelve stalls were provided for the bowlers in York's only hexagonal lavatory at Clarence Gardens in 1902. The facilities for ladies were built 11 years later.

For the next few years the convenience situation in the city remained static, most efforts were directed towards maintenance problems. The urinal in Black Horse Passage, a lane which wove its tortuous way between the houses of Fossgate and the Hungate area, was proving to be a nuisance. To prevent a previous nuisance a slate slab had been erected in 1884 in one of the corners of the passage to form a urinal and a 4ft x 6ft area of sets was let into the cobbles to provide some rudimentary drainage. Unseen and uncared for, the simplest solution for preventing the nuisance here was to remove the offending device. This was done in October 1901 but the probable consequence was that its users would hardly notice it was missing and continue to use the corner with unabated enthusiasm.[64]

While no flushing had been provided here most of the other urinals had a system of a continuous flow of water through a sparge pipe, a horizontal pipe perforated with holes to flush the slate slabs or stalls. This was not only wasteful during the day but more particularly at night when there was no need for it. An automatic flushing system would be more efficient but this could not be done cheaply. The City Engineer was asked to find out the cost of replacing the perforated sparge pipes with roses which could do the same job with less water.[65] Another attempt to save water was the removal of the automatic WC on King's Staithe in 1909.[66] WCs, which were more conspicuous by their absence rather than their presence, were now beginning to be regarded as an essential part of a sanitary convenience. One wonders how the citizens, and the city, had previously fared without an adequate provision of such devices in public places. The sites at both Monk Bar and Micklegate Bar were adapted to provide WCs - two at the former place cost £40 in 1903.[67]

When the management at the Public Library in Clifford Street asked for a lavatory to be provided in the immediate vicinity of their building for the benefit of clients taken short, when choosing a book, it was told, quite firmly, that there were already sufficient nearby. A request that this decision be reconsidered met with equally short shrift. The book borrowers would have to continue to make quick dashes to Tower Street, Parliament Street or King's Staithe, depending on their needs.[68]

The Suburbs

The next stage in the building of public conveniences started in 1907 with demands from the suburbs, first from the South Bank Estate, at this time somewhat isolated from the rest of York by the grounds of Nunthorpe Court which ran right down to Bishopthorpe Road. The house was reached by a lodge gate and entrance drive, later to become South Bank Avenue. The estate was contained between this entrance drive, Bishopthorpe Road, Campleshon Lane and Albemarle Road alongside the Knavesmire. If lavatories were provided here they would serve race-goers, users of the playing fields and dog-strollers as well as the estate itself. Better, if another lavatory was built on Tadcaster Road, the Knavesmire would be well provided for.

The possibilities were many and the City Engineer produced four different schemes for the councillors to consider

1 1 WC and 3 urinal stalls reached from Albemarle Road by seven steps down and from the Knavesmire by six steps up. For those not wishing to visit the lavatory while going from one place to the other a separate flight of steps was to be built - cost £100.
2 1 WC and 3 urinal stalls at the Knavesmire level with a separate flight of steps between Albemarle Road and the Knavesmire - cost £80
3 2 WCs and 6 urinal stalls for men and 2 WCs for women in Tadcaster Road - cost £160.
4 As 3 but less compact and with the entrances less obscured - cost £175.

Not unnaturally the ever prudent councillors, with the ratepayers looking over their shoulders, chose the cheaper scheme for each site.[69]

The chosen site in Albemarle Road was less controversial and, besides, the residents of the area had asked for the facility. It was built by T Belt for £85 11s 0d. In Tadcaster Road the now redundant pinfold opposite Mount Vale was to be used. The residents of Tadcaster Road were largely what Seebohm Rowntree had described as the servant-keeping classes and could not be expected to welcome such a mundane but necessary building on their doorsteps with all the problems which could arise from its use. The Corporation seemed to have realised that consultation would delay or prevent the work and started construction without informing them. When the residents did complain that the building was 'objectionable and a nuisance' the committee decided there was no reason to move it elsewhere and, besides, work had already commenced. The contractor, George Turner, had tendered £197 15s 3d for the construction of this buidling.[70]

Pinfolds, used in earlier times for penning stray animals until they could be released to their owners, were now thought to be suitable places for confining the bursting sportsmen who had replaced the freemen's cattle as users of the strays. The Corporation, having taken over the responsibility for the Knavesmire from the Pasture Masters of Micklegate Stray in 1905, did not have to seek permission to use the pinfold there. However when they proposed to use the pinfold on Monk Stray for a similar purpose they had to negotiate with the Pasture Masters. In 1958, after control of all the other strays had passed to the Corporation, it was agreed that they would be maintained as open spaces for recreation for all time and that no buildings other than sports pavilions, bandstands, public lavatories and other similar places for the convenience of the public, should be erected on them.[71] The Pasture Masters, in agreeing that the pinfold could be used, were only anticipating their successors of half a century hence. However they wanted some acknowledgment for their magnanimity and suggested to the Corporation a rental of £2 a year. The Corporation, however, was made of sterner stuff and retorted that it would only pay 5s 0d a year and then for an initial 21 years lease. The WCs and urinal on the Malton Road were completed in 1912, the original estimate of £62 10s 0d having been exceeded by a third.[72]

The opening of the electric tramway system in York in 1910 seemed like a good opportunity to improve the public lavatory provision in the suburbs. The Tramway management wanted to install conveniences at each of the termini where potential passengers, waiting for a tramcar, would otherwise be tempted to relieve themselves in nearby doorways and gardens to the annoyance of the residents. The Haxby Road terminus was then at Rose Street, just before the railway bridge over the Foss Islands Branch which could not carry the weight of the tramcars. It was used by thousands of Rowntrees employees who walked between the terminus and the factory. This was considered to be a prime site for a waiting room and sanitary convenience. Such a facility could be provided for £150 and the costs shared

The tram drivers and conductors at the original Haxby Road terminus offended the vicar of St Thomas's Church by using his nearby garden as a convenience.

between the Tramway and the Streets and Buildings Committee. The chosen site was the garden of White Cross Lodge which belonged to a third committee, the Education Committee. The stage was set for protracted bureaucratic wrangling. After an inspection in November 1911 by the Reverend W Johnson, Headmaster of Archbishop Holgate's Grammar School, and Dr D Sanderson Long, a medical practitioner and an elected councillor, the scheme was abandoned. The eventual result was a letter of complaint from the Reverend JC Walker, Vicar of St Thomas's whose vicarage was next to the tram terminus. He wrote, in April 1913, that the drivers and conductors were using his garden as a convenience. The ever practical councillors, knowing that mere injunctions would not stop the tramcar crews from performing their natural functions, decided that the solution was to build a urinal there. Luckily for both the councillors and the vicar, the railway bridge was strengthened and Rowntrees factory became an alternative terminus in January 1916.[73] Here the crews must have used lavatories in the factory and at the newly erected dining block. In 1913 the tramway depot on Fulford Road became the only place on the tramway system to get a urinal. This cost £50 and would be used by both the staff who worked there and by members of the general public starting or finishing their journeys there.[74]

The situation at the beginning of 1914 was that men were well provided for with 11 installations with both WCs and urinals and 16 with urinals only. Women on the other hand were catered for only in three places, Silver Street, Haxby Road and the Knavesmire. There was clearly, it was decided, a real necessity for more, not only for female use but, surprisingly, it was thought, for the men as well. Suggested sites were

> Bishopthorpe Road near Balmoral Terrace
> Burton Stone Lane near Haughton Road
> Haxby Road near the Swimming Baths
> Huntington Road near the Railway Bridge
> East Parade on the Glen Estate
> Foss Islands Road near the Corporation Depot
> Hull Road near Green Dykes Lane
> Piccadilly near the New Bridge

which would cost £1050 in total to provide. It was also thought that three of the tram termini, Acomb, Dringhouses, Haxby Road, should be equipped[75] but this was the concern of the Tramways Committee who held its own review. This resulted in the suggestion that a urinal at the Station behind the tram shelter was their first priority, a site which was later to be found objectionable by the Yorkshire Archaeological Society who would not brook any interference with the medieval defences.[76] The declaration of war on 4 August 1914, however, was to bring any consideration of these weighty matters to an end until the hostilities were over and money was again available in the Corporation coffers for civic improvements.

Between the Wars

In 1921 the City Engineer produced his earlier report, made in 1914, but was told that there was no money in the budget and that he would have to defer any plans he had for improving or adding to the conveniences in York until the next year. When he did raise the matter again he was put off for a further year. This was becoming an almost annual routine in the days of financial stringency after the war. In spite of the now pressing need to improve both the ladies' accommodation in Silver Street and the mens' in Parliament Street he was fobbed off again in 1924 and 1925.[77]

Minds were concentrated on the problems by two letters in September 1926. The first was from Councillor WH Shaw who thought that the base of the Waterworks' Tower could easily be converted into facilities for both sexes. The second, from the Reverend RG Pyne, Rector of St Cuthbert's, suggested that another ladies' lavatory was necessary on the south side of the river Ouse. Two sites were available, one on spare ground on the west side of Rougier Street next to the Tramway staff's messroom, and the other on ground to the south-west of the War Memorial Gardens. The City Engineer thought that the latter was the better as it was close to the tramway stopping place, on the principal route for traffic through the city, near to the Station and, finally, not too prominent - in short it would serve a multiplicity of clients.[78] Once again his memory was short. His favoured site had as recently as November 1923 been given to the city by the LNER to mark the very friendly relations which had existed between York and the shortly-to-disappear NER throughout its life. A condition of the gift was that the land was to be laid out and maintained for ever as a public garden and no buildings were to be erected on it.[79] A lavatory block was certainly a building even if it was a 'necessary house'. The Rougier Street site was thus the only alternative and a lavatory for men and a lavatory for women with a permanent attendant was built there in 1927 at a cost of £1,250 granted by the Ministry of Housing. It was recently replaced by new conveniences for both sexes built in Tanner Row in an enclave surrounded by the extension of the General Accident (now CGU) building.[80]

As York's nearest equivalent to a bus station Rougier Street was an important location for public conveniences, seen here to the left of the York West Yorkshire Offices.

Discussion about the facilities in and around Parliament Street had started in 1925 with some inter-committee posturing. The Market Committee, flushed with the success of the Ladies' Cloak Room in Silver Street, proposed that it should make any alterations only to get a flea in the ear from the Streets and Buildings Committee who said that the lavatories were its responsibility and, more importantly, it should continue to take the revenue.[81] The first thoughts were to build new ladies' conveniences behind the shops on the north-west corner of Jubbergate at a cost of £675. This was thought to be an excellent site at a place in the city where there was a great need - moreover it would also serve the summer-time charabanc traffic! The Market Committee preferred to take over the three shops in Silver Street adjacent to the Ladies' Cloak Room, occupied by the Market Superintendent and a bank. For 10 WCs, 8 washbasins, an office for the attendant, a boiler to provide hot water and a turnstile entrance, the cost would be only £620. The Estates Committee, with an eye to the rent revenue to be lost, preferred that the ladies should be given underground facilities alongside the mens' in Parliament Street. While the Jubbergate corner scheme eventually found favour with two of the three committees concerned, the full Council threw it out; the Estates Committee must have been successful in its lobbying of other councillors.[82]

The 1926 sanitary convenience season opened with a new proposal, the ladies' should be built on top of the mens' - a seemingly very practical solution to what was becoming a long running saga. A brick building with a tiled roof was to house the ladies'. Inside the woodwork was to be varnished pitch pine, the partitions glazed bricks, and the walls tiled up to 7ft. The floors were to be laid with patent jointless

To demonstrate the effect of the proposed ladies' lavatory an outline of it has been drawn on a photograph of the construction work then in hand to extend the mens' underground toilet.

impervious material. A contract for the alterations was awarded in October 1926 to HE Turner and Son who had tendered £2,685. But before work was started nimbyism was to triumph again. On 20 January 1927 the local tradesmen led by William Dove, the ironmonger whose shop on the corner of Pavement would overlook the ladies, presented a petition, a protest signed by most of the Parliament Street shopkeepers. The proposed building, 37 ft long, 20 ft wide, 11 ft to the eaves and 19 ft to the ridge, would be a disfigurement and inconvenience (was the pun intended?) to such an important thoroughfare. The height of the building would completely obscure shop names and fascia signs from the opposite side of the street, 'an important factor in competitive business now-a-days'. Finally an above ground building erected where five roads met would increase the danger to pedestrians as vehicles approaching would be completely obscured until too late. A week later it was decided to ignore the petition but successful work behind the scenes resulted in a decision by the Council that

> Any part of the proposed convenience which should appear above the roof of the men's convenience be not constructed

somewhat circumlocutional but, in other words, alterations to the underground men's were all right and if a ladies' was required that too should be built underground.[83]

While the mens' lavatory was being extended it was surrounded by hoardings on which local traders advertised. A sign to tell people what was happening was also included.

A new site was chosen in Parliament Street where it was crossed by Market Street and Jubbergate crossing with entrances at each end in Parliament Street. It was to be constructed so that vehicular traffic could pass unimpeded over the top. On investigation, however, it was found that the existing sewers could not be easily diverted to make way for it - so back to the drawing board once again. Where else was there an unobstructed underground site for the relief of the ladies of York? In June 1927 it was decided that it had to go in St Sampson's Square. It was with much relief that the final plans could now be prepared. There were to be 14 WCs, eight lavatory (wash) basins, a parcel depository under the care of an attendant. Light would come through pavement lights in the flat roof and cast iron gratings would be provided for ventilation. All modern appliances were to be provided in the reinforced concrete shell which was to be lined with Terrazzo. The fish stalls in St Sampson's Square could all be resited so no stall-holders would have to move elsewhere. All this would cost £2,250 or £2,500 if vehicles were to be allowed to drive over the roof.[84]

In September 1927 F Shepherd and Son tendered £2,232 17s 0d for its construction so it was necessary to seek a loan of £2,233 from the Ministry of Health. The Minister directed that a public enquiry be held at the Guildhall on 5 January 1928 before E Butler AMICE. After hearing from his inspector and consulting with the Ministry of Transport the Minister approved the loan in April 1928 and work started immediately. No embarrassing sewers were found during the excavation but Roman remains were - a continuation of the bath buildings which can be seen in the bar of the Roman Bath public house. The new facility opened in 1929.[85]

The charge for the use of a wash basin was to be 2d a person including the use of a towel, but if a personal towel was required another 1d would be charged. The 1d to use a WC would be collected by an automatic lock on each cubicle door. An advertisement in the Press produced 69 applicants for attendants from which the two required were appointed. They would get one week holiday after a year's service. Mrs Dawson was allowed to continue her activities in Silver Street until it was required by the Electricity department who were to install a sub-station there. She died in January 1930 and her daughter took over her tenancy until 30 March.[86]

All this activity had overshadowed the improvements being made to the men's lavatory in 1927. Under the combined ladies'/mens' plan, the old 1894 excavation was to be extended by 22 ft in length and 3 ft in width with entrances and means of lighting at both ends. There were to be 16 urinal stalls, 5 WCs, wash basins with a hot water supply, and a small room for the attendant. This same layout was adopted for the revised scheme without the ladies' on top. At first, like the ladies, it was to be paid for by a Government loan of £1,650 but in the end the costs were met from Council revenue. The attendants in the new underground emporium were to be provided with caps and coats. No roller towels were to be provided for customers. A charge of 2d would include one personal towel while a second towel would cost an extra 1d.

The new convenience at Holgate Beck, an extension of the electricity sub-station.

A new brick public convenience was erected at Holgate Beck in 1929 as an extension to a much larger electricity sub-station. It had a flat roof and was lit by a skylight but it was overshadowed by the pyramidal tiled roof of the sub-station. The new improved lavatory facilities, including both urinals and WCs, cost £350 out of

£905 3s 0d for the whole building which was built by JT Wailes. In 1930 the ladies were given more but certainly not equal consideration by the construction in St George's Field of a very elegant building of red brick relieved with patterns in blue brick and turned stone balusters in the parapet. It had full facilities for both sexes and replaced the urinal in the plantation nearby.[87]

In February 1934 it was suggested that further public conveniences for men were required - in Burton Stone Lane on the slope of the new railway bridge which had replaced the level crossing, in Huntington Road near the railway bridge which carried the Foss Islands branch over the road, in Glen Gardens near one of the entrances from East Parade, Melrosegate near Hull Road shopping centre, on Clifton Green in the bus shelter, in Foss Islands Road at the end of the Corporation Depot. Only one combined facilities for both men and women. This was to be built at the junction of Bishopthorpe Road and Balmoral Terrace. They were estimated to cost £400 each but no funds could be found, not even for just one of them.[88]

Forty years on the 1889 Vespasienne was still catering for the cabbies and other users at Bootham Bar but it had really passed the end of its economic life. There were two alternatives. Should it be removed? If this was done it was hardly likely that the 1929 clients would emulate their predecessors of four decades ago and use a buttress of the Bar for their relief. Alternatively should it be modernised and facilities for ladies added? The City Engineer was asked to report. The only suitable site, a yard behind the arch at the bottom of the steps was occupied by the works of the stone carver, George Walker Milburn. Milburn was willing to give up part of his yard immediately behind the steps but he required his covered workshop there to be replaced. This would cost £90 which, with the provision of 12 urinals and 3 WCs, brought the total cost to £815. It would, of course, only cater for men so the implementation of the scheme was deferred while the City Engineer looked for a site where facilities for both sexes could be found. By July 1930 it was clear that this could not be found so it was decided to go ahead with the mens' convenience only, with a loan from the Ministry of Health. The Ministry provided £745 in 1931 to match the tender of F Shepherd and Son for its construction but would not agree to pay for the alterations to Milburn's workshop. This had to be found elsewhere in the Corporation budget.[89]

While the City Engineer pondered long and hard over the seemingly intractable problem of providing a female convenience near Bootham Bar, a suggestion was received which was to form the basis of the modern policy for public lavatories in York. The North Yorkshire Automobile Club asked if lavatory accommodation could be provided at parking places and bus stopping places. This practical suggestion resulted in notices being displayed near the bus stops in Piccadilly and Exhibition Square, the two principal termini in the City, pointing the way to the nearest convenience and, as a concomitant, the public conveniences were to be more clearly indicated,[90] shades of the coloured glass in the gas lights which had so offended Councillor Pearson at an earlier time!

ORIGINAL FIGURE REFIXED
BY GENERAL CONTRACTOR

CARVED
INSCRIPTN
INCISED
LETTERS

Etty stands on his new plinth, 10ft 2ins high, the ventilating shaft for the facility below.

Then Eureka! With a flash of brilliance the City Engineer realised that there was a space in Exhibition Square that he had not considered. It was right under his nose and, in fact, right under the Etty Memorial which had been unveiled in front of the

Art Gallery in 1911. In September 1935 he proposed to use the Memorial as a central feature, creating a platform round it on which seats could be placed, so arranged that those sitting on them could not watch the entrances to the lavatory at the rear of the monument. An abyss would be excavated underneath Etty for 16 WCs, 12 washbasins and a room for an attendant. To obviate the need for expensive coin-collecting locks on each cubicle door two coin-operated turnstiles would be placed at the entrance to the lavatory section. The whole thing would cost £2,600, only £300 more than that at St Sampson's Square.[91]

The councillors were delighted with the ingenuity of their engineer and fully supported his scheme which required Etty to be placed on top of a new plinth 10ft 2ins high which was, in fact, the ventilation shaft for the convenience below. What Etty, in his day a fierce guardian of the antiquities of his birthplace, would have thought is best left to the imagination. When fighting to preserve the walls that were under threat of demolition he had said

> Beware how you destroy your antiquities, guard them with religious care. They are what give you a decided character and superiority over other provincial cities. You have lost much, take care of what remains.

but a lavatory under his statue, however much a necessity, was surely an act of vandalism. He would, no doubt, have been supported in his opinions by the many potential users of the facility, who would have to struggle down the steps, carrying a couple of heavy bags of shopping, fumble in their purses to try and locate the necessary penny to put in the slot before making the effort to squeeze through the revolving gates. Happily for them another war was to intervene and afterwards another site became available, Milburn's Yard, reached through an arch in the city wall. Would the present day citizens of York have preferred it to the different type of fountain which has played, somewhat intermittently and sometimes full of foaming washing-up liquid, in front of William Etty since 1971?

Acomb was brought within York's boundary in 1937 to the regret of many of its inhabitants who did not want to pay the increased rates that their new local authority was to charge them. Perhaps as a sop to the new reluctant rate-payers a plan was prepared in 1938 to provide both men and women's conveniences at the junction of Wetherby Road and Front Street. For £876 seven WCs and an attendant's room could be provided for the women and two WCs and six urinals for the men. The land did not belong to the Corporation so the Town Clerk was instructed to negotiate for it but not to pay more than £125.[92] Again the intervention of the Second World War frustrated the provision of a much needed facility.

Fifty-five Years of Peace

The years of austerity were to extend for some ten years after victory. Building materials were scarce and licences were necessary to obtain them. It was not until 1954 that the councillor's thoughts could turn, once again, to toilets and Acomb was foremost in these thoughts. Inflation had taken its toll and the cost was now estimated to be £1,113, less than a ½d on the rates. The new convenience was completed by the beginning of 1955 and soon became a target for vandalism. To prevent damage of the sort that occurred in May the solution, enigmatically, was to erect a wire 'above the door to prevent entry'. This may have prevented further occurrences of the particular problem but the vandals continued to target the Acomb convenience and cause considerable damage. When the accounts were closed in 1956 it was found that the total cost was £1,256, the estimate had been exceeded by £143, the Ministry of Housing and Local Government had to be asked for an additional loan.[93]

The public lavatory at Acomb built in 1955, alongside 3As shop, and closed in March 1990. It was demolished shortly afterwards.

Clifton was another suburb without such facilities and in 1954 it was proposed that part of the bus shelter, originally a charging station for the battery operated buses which used to run between Clifton and the Market Place, should be converted into toilets for both sexes. However another site, near Clifton Green, was found but negotiations failed to secure it.[94] It was thus 34 years before Clifton was to get its first public convenience. After closing time pub customers were using doorways and lanes so a petition was organised. Twelve hundred names were collected; only two people refused to sign. Faced with such a well supported demand the Corporation let a contract to William Birch and Sons in 1988 to convert the whole of the bus shelter into male, female and disabled facilities at a cost of nearly £32,000. Additionally an all-night toilet was provided for those caught short when the rest of the building was closed at 8pm. All the units contained 'the new hand wash system which is totally vandal proof'![95] However necessary it was, it was closed in March 1995 to save £4,000 a year. Its usage was, according to the Director of Environmental Services, so small that it was uneconomical to maintain it. Nevertheless the landlord of the Old Grey Mare has noticed a considerable increase of people coming into his pub with only one purpose in mind - one which did not increase his profits![96]

The Electrobus charging station and bus shelter at Clifton Green before it was converted into a public convenience.

With the impetus of toilet building restored, plans were made to provide conveniences in Lord Mayor's Walk and Melrosegate in 1956 and Knavesmire Road and Fulford Road in 1957 - the first three for males and females and the last for males only. This was somewhat ambitious and progress was much slower. Melrosegate got its facility in 1957, based on the Acomb model. It was built by D Hughes of Danebury Drive for £1,373 13s 10d.[97] A report on the poor condition of the ladies' convenience in Mount Vale provided the catalyst for the Knavesmire Road scheme in September 1958 which was to replace both Mount Vale and Albemarle Road. Three years were to pass before a spade was put into the ground. When the proposal was advertised in the local newspapers objections were received from the residents of Trentholme Drive. Nevertheless on practical considerations it was decided to go ahead; a convenience to serve the Knavesmire, with all its leisure activity, was essential and one placed between the race-course and the playing fields was ideally sited to meet the needs of most of the visitors there.[98]

Ladies were given a lavatory at the bottom of Holgate Hill in 1965, 36 years after the gentlemen were given theirs. The new ladies', adjacent to the gentlemen's, and incorporating a public shelter, was built by Claxton and Garland for £1,705 14s 0d.[99]

The shopkeepers in Spurriergate did not really appreciate the presence of the urinal in Church Lane. When Salisbury's Handbags, the purchasers of 12-16 Spurriergate, its immediate neighbour, were making their plans for alterations to the shop in 1957 they asked the Corporation if the urinal could be closed or moved. 'We would be only too happy' replied the Corporation ' provided that an alternative convenience is provided at your expense'. Needless to say it remained, in unhappy proximity to Salisbury's.[100] The situation was saved in 1966 when the shop next to Ouse Bridge in Low Ousegate was conveyed to the Provincial Building Society. In return for this favour the Building Society agreed to incorporate on the lower floor of their new building the shell of a public convenience which would not only replace the offending and, no doubt offensive, one in Church Lane but would also allow WCs to be provided for both sexes. Further it would allow the Corporation to rent it for a peppercorn, £5 a year, on a 21 year lease. The shell was equipped for its purpose at a cost of £8,250. It was opened with great acclaim -'The first newly built toilets for many years', the press had conveniently forgotten the very recent developments in the suburbs, but sufficient care had not been taken in its planning. It was unsupervised and its entrance was out of general public view. Vandalism and vice were uncontrollable . There was only one solution - it had to be closed.[101]

At this time St George's Field was tarmacked to cater for ever increasing demands of the motor car and its users, the 1929 building was suitably converted for the sole use of ladies and a new, less ambitious, building was provided for men. More recently, in 1994, these two buildings have in turn been replaced to make way for the new pumping station, part of York's flood defences.

In 1968 £5,000 was earmarked for the building of a new public convenience at one of three sites; Malton Road, to replace the old convenience in the pinfold, Nunnery Lane Car Park, Wigginton Road, to replace the older convenience in Haxby Road. In fact, they were all built in spite of an objection from the Pasture Masters of Monk Stray against the one to be erected in a lay-by opposite the Herdsman's Cottage on the stray. Claxton and Garland erected the buildings at Malton Road and Wigginton Road, having tendered £5,621 and £6,024 17s 0d respectively.[102]

The urinal on the Esplanade had provided relief for male riverside walkers until 1975 when construction on a new toilet block for all sexes was started just inside the Museum Gardens with an entrance gate from the Esplanade.[103] The Yorkshire Philosophical Society, the owner of the Museum Gardens, had objected to the urinal at the time of its opening in 1890 but the Museum Gardens had been handed over, first in 1961 to York Corporation, and then in 1974, to North Yorkshire County

Council. Objections to a facility that was to serve a much wider hinterland were thus stifled at birth. It has been serving its useful and necessary purpose, more unobtrusively than most, since 1977.

A period of slow growth was now to be followed by retrenchment. Some were now little used; most suffered from vandalism; the cost of supervision, maintenance and repair were escalating; all these factors determined the fate of some of the old urinals as well as some very recently built public conveniences. Seven were proposed for closure in 1976, Baile Hill, Blue Bridge Lane, Dennis Street, Fourth Avenue, Melrosegate, Micklegate Bar, Walmgate Bar, but before this could be done the users were informed of the Corporation's intentions through an advertisement in the local newspapers. A three month period was allowed in which objections could be made. Surprisingly in view of the uproar that normally follows a proposal for change, only eight objections were received. One of the seven urinals to be closed must have had at least two friends! As a sop the Council had proposed to make improvements to the closed sites. At Baile Hill the area was to be paved and a seat provided for those earlier users to take their ease and ponder over happier times spent there but nothing has been done. The users of most of the closed sites had to walk further for their relief. Only the old convenience at Micklegate Bar had an alternative facility nearby, the much more luxurious and newly provided building in Nunnery Lane Car Park. The relentless march of the internal combustion engine was progressing apace. The new visitors to York no longer used Shanks's mare. The official closure date, 12 April 1976, for the seven sites went by unnoticed. To mourn for *necessaria* was obviously undignified.[104] The Monk Bar convenience escaped this purge and was even proposed for refurbishment in 1981 but it was cheaper to close it. All other urinal only sites have since been closed.

It was the motor car which was to dictate future policy for the provision of public conveniences in York - only a small change to that of the Victorian fathers of the city. They had placed urinals at all the entrances to the city to be used by citizens and visitors who used their legs more than any other form of transport. In the late 20th century legs have become almost redundant. Most visitors now arrive in their personal transport so nearly all new conveniences have been built in car parks, the new entrances to the city - in Lord Mayor's Walk adjacent to St John Street car park, Clarence Street (at both St John's and Union Terrace car parks), Coppergate (1982), Foss Bank (1984) and Kent Street. The latter which opened in November 1990 cost £95,000.[105] (Compare that with £14 10s 0d for the urinal built on South Esplanade in 1848). It, of course, has all the latest user-friendly and vandal-proof lavatory technology which, naturally, includes a baby changing facility. This phrase conjures up visions of parents with disorderly and rebellious children bringing them to Kent Street in the hope that they will be able to swap them for something more amenable. In recognition of this ambiguous meaning later signs say BABYCARE.

In 1986 the Corporation was faced with the prospect of spending £120,000 on refurbishing the two underground conveniences in the city centre. This was on top of its annual budget of £211,000 for maintaining 18 public lavatories in York. One of the alternatives considered was the provision of up to eight 'superloos' instead of the underground facilities. These devices cost £25,000 each and provided wash basins, vanity mirrors, automatically set water temperatures, piped music and were self cleaned after each use. For 'safety' reasons the door would burst open after 15 minutes occupancy and the unwitting user would be exposed to public view - better this than being inside during the self cleaning routine! While it was agreed in principle to provide autoloos to supplement the conventional lavatories in the city nothing was to be done until a public lavatory policy was drawn up, to cover sites, signposting, facilities for the disabled, and charges. This was, however, overtaken by other events in the city centre.[106]

From 1836 until 1964, when the last few stalls were transferred to Newgate, Parliament Street was York's market place. Then, devoid of this obstruction, the traffic on the A19, an important route through the centre of York, could flow more freely. The provision of an inner ring road and the construction of an outer by-pass, which was finally completed in 1987, allowed the diversion of traffic from the city centre and the creation of footstreets in its historic core. A report entitled *A City for the Pedestrian* had been published in the previous year and it contained the idea that Parliament Street should be included in the pedestrianisation. A competition was launched in 1989 by the Royal Institute of British Architects and the Corporation jointly to find a design which would make this street the centrepiece of the footstreet system. Thirty-seven designs were received which, by the beginning of 1990, had been reduced to seven from which a final shortlist of three was to be selected before the opinions of the citizens of York were sought. The winner was Sir Charles Nicholsons' Group but inevitably the final plan for the street was a watered down version of the Group's proposal.[107]

All the designers had had to deal with the problem of the underground conveniences. Given the declared themes of simplicity, light and colour the choice of such a large building, a pastiche of several architectural styles, dominating the Piccadilly end of the street, seemed peculiar. It was claimed that its bulk provided a very necessary wind break to a long open thoroughfare. It was sited over the old underground gentlemen's lavatory which was suitably refurbished. The ground floor contains the ladies', replacing that in St Sampson's Square, and in the gable is the office of the City Centre Superintendent who can supervise the comings and goings of toilet users without leaving his desk. This £270,000 development caused considerable controversy, perhaps best summed up by Pennie Calder writing a letter to the editor of the *Yorkshire Evening Press* on 17 October 1991

> Having read in the Evening Press how much improved York's Parliament street now looks, especially with the temporary resiting of the market there, I decided to go and have a look last week.
>
> It certainly did all look rather jolly in the sunshine - a vast improvement on the' fast food' wagons and the bike park. Then I walked a bit further - to

opposite Marks and Spencer in fact - and I was amazed to see a very large red building rising up at great speed. What could it be? Maybe the Mansion House was being resited as the final 'jewel in the crown' of Parliament Street. When I read the explanatory notice I was truly amazed - a public lavatory no less! This really must be the 'carbuncle' to beat all!

The 'splash palace' in Parliament Street, shades of the Chalet de Necessité *proposed and rejected over 100 years previously.*

I know it is important to have good, modern, clean facilities particularly in a tourist town, but surely a refurbishment of the existing underground ones would have been a more sympathetic idea. If it was thought necessary to build such a large unattractive building there must be a less unobtrusive site - what about the Stonegate Arcade, for example, as it has very little other use and is very central.

I am amazed that the Civic Trust has not made any comment; they usually have plenty to say about unsightly shop signs in Parliament Street and this building is much worse.

No, it seems as if York is about to become the Clochemerle of England! I only hope that it is not with similar consequences.[108]

This comment came too late but it is remarkable that the 'splash palace', as it was nick-named, occasioned so little opprobrium from the shopkeepers in its vicinity. On all the previous occasions when urinals and WCs were being built in this area the Corporation was bombarded with petitions in opposition. Perhaps the difference was that the surrounding shops were now all branches of national multiples whose remote management did not have the same feeling for their locality as did their

Shortly after the Second World War, Milburn's Yard became available and a Ladies' lavatory, reached by the door under the circular arch, was built there. At the same time the Gents' was rebuilt behind the steps.

predecessors who were citizens as well as shopkeepers and, in any case, would see the users attracted by the facilities as potential customers at their emporia.

In place of the ladies' lavatory in St Sampson's Square a new lavatory, with access at street level, was erected for the disabled. It, too, is built in the same architectural style as its fellow at the opposite end of Parliament Street. The redesigned street was opened on 30 April 1992 by Councillor Bob Fletcher, chairman of the planning committee, and Hugh Bayley, MP for York.[109] It is a pity that the lord mayor was not there. The official party could then have made a ceremonial performance in the 'splash palace' after which the MP could have pulled the lord mayor's chain - a suggestion which the Earl of Scarbrough made to the Mayor of Sheffield when opening a sewage treatment works near Roche Abbey.

The high cost of buildings, maintenance, repairs after vandalism, and the provision of attendance at public conveniences have all had an effect on the Corporation's lavatorial policy. Facilities were only kept at those places where the need was clearly demonstrable but then in 1992 a new enemy to public lavatories appeared from an unexpected quarter - the valuation officer. After revaluation in March 1992 the bill for non-domestic rates on conveniences in York was £29,440, an increase of £12,650. The rateable value of the lavatories in Nunnery Lane had risen by 570% to £7,700, the same as the new building in Parliament Street, while Foss Bank was rated at £8,200. Appeals were lodged but the Corporation had no alternative but to pay. The increased demand had come, said one councillor, at a time when the Council was not exactly flush with cash. But worse was to come in 1993. To make ends meet the lavatories at Heworth Green car park (temporary), Foss Bank, Holgate Road (demolished 1999) and Malton Road were all to be closed at the beginning of April, a package which would save £28,650 annually. The Wigginton Road convenience was to be opened for only six months each year in the summer and the opening hours at Parliament Street, Coppergate and Exhibition Square were to be reduced.[110]

Since then the Malton Road lavatory has been severely damaged when it was hit by a road vehicle and, to prevent vandalism, it has been demolished. But happier news was on the horizon for the Wigginton Road convenience which had meanwhile been totally closed. The bowlers who used the greens in Clarence Gardens asked the Corporation if the building could be re-opened for their sole use. Five thousand pounds were spent on repairs in 1995 and alterations before the ownership of the building was transferred from environmental services to leisure services. At least the building and its equipment are still there and can be recommissioned for public use if the demand rises once again.[111]

Further closures, Haxby (now within York's boundary), Acomb (rebuilt nearby and opened in April 1990), Knavesmire and Lord Mayor's Walk, were proposed in April 1997 to save £32,000 annually.[112] Haxby was reprieved by the parish council agreeing to take over the annual running costs of £4,200 and Acomb was eventually reopened, financed by the neighbourhood forums in the area.[113] Then, miraculously, Lord Mayor's Walk was reopened on 4 July 1998 as a private enterprise venture by Janet Kitchen who had spent a day sitting outside the closed facility and had found that many people were desperate to use it.[114] Unfortunately, on 26 September, just three months later Mrs Kitchen's brave enterprise failed. Fewer people were using the nearby car park and those that did were unhappy with her charge of 20p to use the premises.[115]

The current situation is that York now has just 13 public conveniences (see below), six in the city centre (one for the exclusive use of the disabled), five in car or coach parks, and just two in the suburbs. This is a far cry from the heady days of the 19th century. Whether this is adequate for a city which relies on its visitors for its well-being, only time will tell, but what is certain is that the need will always be there unless the human race can be genetically re-engineered.

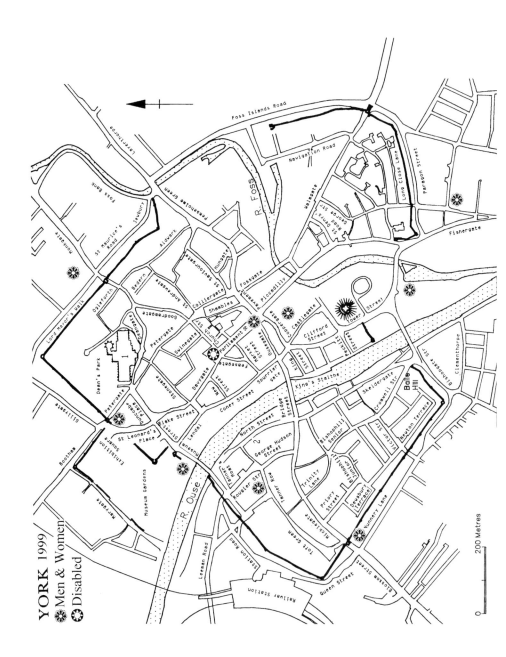

YORK 1999/
❀ Men & Women
✪ Disabled

200 Metres

0

Public Conveniences in York (November 1998)

Location	Normal hours
Clarence Street, St John's Coach Park	Available 24 hours
Clarence Street, Union Terrace Car Park	8.00am-8.00pm
Coppergate Shopping Centre*	8.00am-8.00pm
Exhibition Square (St Leonard's Place)*†§	8.00am-8.00pm
Haxby*†	8.00am-8.00pm
Kent Street Car Park*†	8.00am-8.00pm
Museum Gardens*†	8.00am-8.00pm
Nunnery Lane Car Park*†	8.00am-8.00pm
Parliament Street*	8.00am-8.00pm
St George's Field Car Park*†	8.00am-8.00pm
St Sampson's Square (disabled only)	Available 24 hours
Tanner Row*†	8.00am-8.00pm
York Road, Acomb*†	8.00am-8.00pm

All sites have toilets for the disabled. After normal closing time they can all, except that at Exhibition Square (St Leonard's Place), be opened by a universal key supplied by the Royal Association for Disability and Rehabilitation (RADAR).

* Parent and baby facilities
† Special all-night toilet available
§ Disabled toilet only accessible 8.00am-8.00pm

ACKNOWLEDGEMENTS

As ever my thanks are due to Rita Freedman and her staff in the City Archives and Amanda Howard and the staff in the Reference Library for their unfailing courtesy when searching in their collections to find the documents and newspapers which I needed to consult in the production of this work. My gratitude is also due to Van Wilson and Mike Race for undertaking the editorial and production tasks which have resulted in my researches being made public.

ILLUSTRATIONS

The illustrations on pages 7, 8, 12, 18, 20, 22, 24, 26, 30, 40 are reproduced by kind permission of York City Archives and the lower picture on page 1 the York Archaelogical Trust. The remainder are from the author's collection.

APPENDIX 1

LAVATORY ATTENDANTS & NIGHT SOIL WORKERS WAGES

On 14 July 1908 a deputation of Corporation workmen submitted a claim for increased wages, supported by a comprehensive list of comparative figures from other towns and cities. The City Engineer was asked to make enquiries to confirm this information and he reported his findings to the Streets and Buildings Committee on 15 December 1908. For information on lavatory attendants he had approached nine northern towns, Darlington, Gateshead, Middlesborough, Newcastle, Stockton, South Shields, Sunderland, Tynemouth and West Hartlepool, while for other employees he made his survey in 34 provincial towns throughout the country. He found the following hourly rates:

Lavatory Attendants

			York		
Max	Min	Average	Max	Min	Average
5.70d	4.80d	5.34d	5.00d	4.75d	4.87d
S Shields	W Hartlepool	6 towns			

Night soil men

Max	Min	Average	
6.76d	5.75d	6.11d	6.00d - no other rate
Burton on Trent	Coventry	8 towns	

Night soil carters

Max	Min	Average	
6.25d	4.03d	5.15d	5.50d - no other rate
Leeds	Colchester	31 towns	

The committee members were relieved to find that, while York was below average, it was paying its employees as a whole above the minimum. Having considered the list and looked at the position thereon occupied by York it concluded that the time was not opportune nor justifiable for recommending any advancement of the wages of its workmen.

APPENDIX 2 - NECESSARY WORDS

Over the centuries there has been a reluctance to call a spade a spade in the matter of the name for the place where basic human needs have to be met. 'Grundyism' has removed some words from polite use and substituted others which in their turn have suffered the same fate. The list below has been culled from the *Oxford English Dictionary*. An additional list could equally be compiled for those phrases used, especially within the confines of a family, to explain a person's need to disappear for a short while, including, heard on the BBC, 'I'm just going to turn the vicar's bicycle round'.

back-house	geography	necessary vault	shouse
backside	ginger-bread office	netty	siege
bathroom	gong	night-chair	siege-hole
bench-hole	head/s	night-table	siege-house
bog-house	hers	office	smallest room
boggard	his	outhouse	stall
can	his and hers	pan	stool
chaise percée	house	passage-house	stool of ease
chalet	house of ease	petty	stool of easement
chamber	house of easement	piss-house	suite
chamber pot	house of office	pissery	tea room
chapel	issue	pissing-place	thinking place
cloaca	jakes	pissing-post	throne
cloak-room	jerry	pissoir	thunder box
closet	John	place	toilet
closet of ease	jordan	plumbing	two-holer
comfort station	ladies' cloakroom	pot	urinal
common house	lat.	potty	urinary
commons	latrine	privy	urinette
commode	lav.	privy house	urinoir
convenience	lavatory	purging place	usual office/s
coole-hole	little boys' room	quarter gallery	vault
cottage	little girls' room	rear/s	vespasienne
crap-house	little house	recess	wardrobe
crapper	long-house	rere-dorter	washdown
crapping case	loo	rest room	washroom
dike, dyke	lords	retreat	water-closet
draught	men's	seat of ease	WC
draught-house	men's room	set-bowl	withdraught
dunny	Miss White	shield	woodshed
Elsan	necessary house	shit-house	
garden-house	necessary place	shiter	
garderobe	necessary stool	shitter	

NOTES

1. Raine, A., *Mediaeval York* (1955) p213;
   YCA D1 f6b.
2. T.P. Cooper *Lights o' York* (n.d.) p8.
3. Raine A. (ed), *York Civic Records, Vol 4* (1945) Yorkshire Archaeological Society Record Series Vol. 108, p. 122;
   YCA B27 fo 228b.
4. York City Archives (YCA) C91 Bridgemaster's Roll, Ouse Bridge 1584.
5. YCA, CS, Chamberlain's Books of Account, 1584/5, f65v.
6. Raine, *op. cit.* in note 1, p55.
7. Raine, *op. cit.* in note 1, p189.
8. YCA, B33 ff63 & 66.
9. YCA, C25 f16v; c29 f31; B41 f197-197v.
10. YCA, B33 f250.
11. YCA, B42 p142.
12. *York Courant* 1754.
13. YCA, Assembly Room Directors' Minute Book 1730-58 p290.
14. YCA, BC 712 Ouse Navigation Committee Minutes p20, 26, 27 & 38.
15. Davison A. 'A Genuine and Superior Article: the last two centuries of Brewing in York', *York Historian 10* (1992) p 39;
    Peacock A. *York 1900-1914* (n.d. but 1992) p26.
16. YCA, BC7/2 pp21, 26, 99, & 103.
17. YCA BC7/2 8 Aug 1851, 8 October 1852, 6 July 1854, 24 June 1856;
    YCA BC16/5 pp 324 & 449;
    YCA BC17/3 p 59;
    YCA BB4 Local Board of Health Committee Minutes p 278;
    YCA Streets and Buildings Committee 21 April 1892.
18. W. Giles *York: City Walls, Gates, Posterns, Ramparts and Ditches,* Mss collection, York Reference Library, Vol 2.
19. YCA BB6 8 September, 3 & 9 November 1857.
20. YCA Sanitary Committee 14 & 21 August 1866
21. R. Reynolds *Cleanliness and Godliness* (1943) p32.
22. P Howard 'A Taxonomy of Imposters', *The Times* 22 March 1991 p16.
23. YCA   Sanitary Committee 27 February, 26 March & 4 June 1889;
    Streets and Buildings Committee, 30 July, 12 & 26 November,
    3 December 1889.
24. YCA Council Meeting 6 Jan, 18 February, 13 March 1890.
25. YCA Streets and Buildings Street Committee 10 April 1894.
26. YCA Sanitary Committee 17 October, 28 November 1865.
27. YCA Streets and Building Committee 24 November 1903, 29 March 1904.
28. YCA Sanitary Committee 17 October, 28 November 1865.
29. YCA Estates Committee BC 24/1 13 April, 11 May 1887.
30. YCA Estates Committee BC24/1 25 January 1888.
31. YCA Estates Committee BC24/2 19 February 1889.
32. YCA House Books BB5, 14, 21 March 1854; BB6 5, 12, 26 July 1859.

33. YCA Urban Sanitary Committee BC17/1 24 December 1872, 28 January 1873.
34. YCA Streets and Buildings Committee 15 March 1892.
35. YCA Local Board of Health BC16, various dates 14 April 1865 to 29 September 1868.
36. YCA Urban Sanitary Committee BC17/1 4 July 1871.
37. YCA Urban Sanitary Committee BC17/1 28 October 1873.
38. YCA Urban Sanitary Committee BC17/5 2 & 16 November, 28 December 1880.
39. YCA Streets and Buildings Committee 10 June, 2 September 1890, 12 May 1891, 6 Dec 1892, 4 July 1893.
40. G. Warren *Vanishing Street Furniture* (1979) p67 et seq.
41. YCA Streets and Buildings Committee 21 November, 4 December 1893, 22 May 1894, 9 March 1909.
42. YCA Markets Committee BC2/5 21 February, 17 April 1896.
43. YCA Markets Committee BC2/5 10 July, 4 September, 2 October 1896, 19 March 1897.
44. YCA Markets Committee 27 November 1896.
45. YCA Streets and Buildings Committee 15, 26 May, 23 June 1896
46. YCA Council 13 July 1896.
47. YCA Streets and Buildings Committee 19 January, 20 July, 9 August 1897; Market Committee 1 February 1897.
48. YCA Streets and Buildings Committee 12 Oct 1897.
49. YCA Streets and Buildings Committee 30 November, 14 December 1897, 7 June, 11 July 1898.
50. 2nd Annual Report of City Engineer and Surveyor for year ended 31 March 1913 (1914) p17.
51. YCA Streets and Buildings Committee BC25/1 2 October 1888.
52. YCA Streets and Buildings Committee BC21/51 5 February 1889, 14 October 1890;
    YCA Estates Committee BC18/1 30 January 1889.
53. YCA Streets and Buildings Committee 4 July, 4 October 1910.
54. YCA Estates Committee BC24/1 5 September, 17, 31 October, 28 November 1888.
55. YCA Streets and Buildings Committee BC25 10 April, 23 October, 4 December 1894, 15 Jan 1895.
56. YCA Streets and Buildings Committee BC25 9 April 1895, 5 Jan 1897.
57. J. Smith *Report to the General Board of Health on a Preliminary Enquiry into the Sewerage, Drainage and Supply of Water, and the Sanitary Conditions of the Inhabitants of the City of York* (1850).
58. YCA Streets and Buildings Committee BC25/5 27 December 1899, 5 February 1900;
    BC25/6.
59. YCA Health Committee 2 July 1900.
    YCA Streets and Buildings Committee BC25/7 28 October 1902.
60. L. Lambton *Temples of Convenience* (1878) pl 47 and 48.
61. B S Rowntree *Poverty* (1902) p308.

62. YCA Streets and Buildings Committee 10 July, 13 August, 18 September, 16 October, 13 November 1900.
    YCA Estates Committee BC24/2 25 October 1900.
63. YCA Estates Committee BC24/2 21 June, 15 July, 19 August, 2 September 1901, 16 June 1902, 16 July, 10 September 1912, 7 April 1913;
    YCA Parks Committee 17 July 1925.
64. YCA Sanitary Committee BC/17/6 14 October 1883.
    YCA Streets and Buildings Committee BC25/6 15 October 1901.
65. YCA Streets and Committee BC25/6 18 March 1902.
66. YCA Streets and Buildings Committee 23 March 1909.
67. YCA Streets and Buildings Committee 8 December 1903.
68. YCA Streets and Buildings Committee 1 August, 29 August 1905.
69. YCA Streets and Buildings Committee 4 January 1909.
70. YCA Streets and Buildings Committee BC25/10 19 June, 24 August 1909.
71. York Group for the Promotion of Planning *The Strays and Ways of York* (1968) p5.
72. YCA Streets and Buildings Committee BC25/7 7, 21 September 1909, 31 May, 4 October 1910, 5 September 1991, 6 February, 23 April 1912.
73. YCA Tramways Committee 5 September, 3 October 1911, 8 April 1913;
    YCA Streets and Buildings Committee 14 November 1911;
    YCA Sites Sub-committee 20 November, 11, 30 December 1911;
    YCA Education Committee 20 October 1911.
74. YCA Streets and Buildings Committee 2 February, 9 September 1913.
75. YCA Streets and Buildings Committee 6 January, 14 August 1914.
76. YCA Streets and Buildings Committee 8 December 1914, 27 April 1927.
77. YCA Streets and Buildings Committee 15 November 1921, 10 January, 14 February 1922, 11 November 1924.
78. YCA Streets and Buildings Committee 14 September, 9 November 1926.
79. H Murray *Dr Evelyn's York* (1983) pp40/1.
80. YCA Streets and Buildings Committee 15 March, 10 May 1927.
81. YCA Streets and Buildings Committee 9 June 1925.
82. YCA Markets Committee March 1925;
    YCA Streets and Buildings Committee 17 April, 8 May, 5 June, 10 July 1925.
83. YCA Streets and Buildings Committee 13 April 1926, 27 January, 4 April 1927.
84. YCA Streets and Buildings Committee 12 April, 13, 14, 21 June 1927;
    YCA Markets Committee BC2/7 9 March 1927.
85. YCA Streets and Buildings Committee 13 September, 13 December 1927, 13 March, 24 April 1928.

86. YCA Streets and Buildings Committee 6 May, 14 May 1929, 10 January 1930.
87. YCA Streets and Buildings Committee 13 April 1926, 15 March, 4 April, 13 September, 15 November, 13 December 1927.
88. YCA Streets and Buildings Committee 15 July 1924, 9 April, 9 July 1929, 10, 20 September 1929.
89. YCA Acc 191 Pigeon Hole 329.

90. YCA Streets and Buildings Committee 9 April , 14 May, 9 July, 12 November 1929, 15 July, 11 November 1930, 10 February, 9 June, 15 September 1931.

91. YCA Streets and Buildings Committee 10 April 1934.

92. YCA Drainage and Sanitary Act Committee BC14 p94;
    YCA Streets and Buildings Committee 10 September 1935.

93. YCA Streets and Buildings Committee BC25/14 12 April 1938.

94. YCA Streets and Buildings Committee 15 June 1954, 10 May, 2 December 1955, 2 March, 14 September 1956.

95. YCA Streets and Buildings Committee 2 September 1954, 11 January 1955.

96. *Yorkshire Evening Press* 14 June 1988.

97. *Yorkshire Evening Press* 7 March 1995.

98. YCA Streets and Buildings Committee 2 September 1954, 11, 28 September 1956, 12 March, 30 August 1957.

99. YCA Streets and Buildings Committee 2 September 1968, 4 September 1961.

100. YCA Streets and Buildings Committee 14 April, 13 October 1964, 28 May 1965.

101. YCA Streets and Buildings Committee 17 December 1957.

102. YCA Council 7 February 1966;
     Yorkshire Evening Press 21 December 1968.

103. YCA Streets and Buildings Committee 24 May, 10 September 1968, 11 February, 11 March, 20 October 1969 and 13 October 1970.

104. *Yorkshire Evening Press* 22 October 1975.

105. *Yorkshire Evening Press* 4 November, 4 December 1975, 7 April 1976.

106. *Yorkshire Evening Press* 10 November 1970.

107. *Yorkshire Evening Press* 21 October 1986.

108. *Yorkshire Evening Press* 25 January 1990.

109. *Yorkshire Evening Press* 17 October 1991.

110. *Yorkshire Evening Press* 30 April 1992.

111. *Yorkshire Evening Press* 18 December 1992, 12, 17 February 1993.

112. *Yorkshire Evening Press* 13 October 1994, 15 March, 20 April 1995.

113. *Yorkshire Evening Press* 9 April 1997.

114. *York Advertiser* 29 May 1997.

115. *Yorkshire Evening Press* 4 July 1998.

116. *Yorkshire Evening Press* 29 September 1998.